iews of the Original Edition

"This book is a "MUST READ" for anyone directly involved with children. As the mother of four sons that have been the victims of sexual abuse, I recommend this book to all victims and their families."

AUG − − 2006   —*Susan J. Lock, Ohio*

"If you want to keep your children safe from sexual predators, you NEED this book! It is the most important book you will ever read."
—*Lillyth Denaghy Keogh, Mother and former victim*

"My brother spent seven years in prison for child molestation. I highly recommend this book for anyone who has someone like that in their own family."

—*Jim F.*

"This is an extremely important, groundbreaking book. His voice comes from an altogether unexpected quarter: the voice of the sexual predator himself and it is a compelling and urgent voice. It is absolutely critical that we listen."
—Joy Helmer, *former Group Leader, Washington State Prison*

"By focusing on free will, Goldenflame has restored sex offenders to the status of human beings. By focusing on the need for penitence and public identification, he has set the terms for their re-entry into society. By focusing on their immense talent for deception, he has warned us why we must remain ever vigilant. Altogether a remarkable book, full of common sense in a subject-area long in need of it."
—*Link Byfield, chairman of the Citizens Centre for Freedom and Democracy, Edmonton, Alberta, Canada.*

"Profound, practical, '   original, the solutions in this book
—*Cand*   *wsmagazine*

D1337866

OVERCOMING SEXUAL TERRORISM

OVERCOMING SEXUAL TERRORISM

60 Ways to Protect Your Children from Sexual Predators

Jake Goldenflame

iUniverse, Inc.

New York   Lincoln   Shanghai

OVERCOMING SEXUAL TERRORISM
60 Ways to Protect Your Children from Sexual Predators

Copyright © 2006 by Jake Goldenflame

iUniverse books may be ordered through booksellers or by contacting:

iUniverse
2021 Pine Lake Road, Suite 100
Lincoln, NE 68512
www.iuniverse.com
1-800-Authors (1-800-288-4677)

All profits from the sale of this book will go to the author's continuing charitable projects in the reduction of sexual abuse worldwide through public education, victim assistance, community crisis intervention and offender reform.

Cover graphic by Doris M. Bleier

ISBN-13: 978-0-595-38355-9 (pbk)
ISBN-13: 978-0-595-67613-2 (cloth)
ISBN-13: 978-0-595-82728-2 (ebk)
ISBN-10: 0-595-38355-6 (pbk)
ISBN-10: 0-595-67613-8 (cloth)
ISBN-10: 0-595-82728-4 (ebk)

Printed in the United States of America

Contents

ACKNOWLEDGMENTS

A number of people have helped in the creation of this edition, ranging from former victims to former offenders, family members of both, members of the treatment community, the legal community, law enforcement and community corrections, as well as readers of the original edition who have been kind enough to write me.

I particularly thank Attorney Mary Lisa Sullivan for generously investing so much of her time in reading over the manuscript to guide me in making needed corrections in its punctuation, grammar and syntax. If any were missed, they're my fault. Her encouragement of my work is deeply valued.

Public Health Service Psychotherapist John McFadden is owed a special debt of thanks for having helped me review my own dark journey of 25 years ago in greater depth and with greater understanding. A number of our findings have been added to this edition.

I also thank the media, which has been the midwife of this book, first suggesting that its original edition be written and then, through its relentless questioning and probing, causing me to unearth even deeper foundations for my recovery which I've included in this edition.

My gratitude goes to all of the above for sharing their skills, experience and knowledge but I, alone, am responsible for how accurately I have told what they have taught me. As I said in the book's first introduction: *may our journeys heal others.*

NOTE

In the interest of fair notice, readers should know that an attorney has advised me that records could not be found for an arrest reported on pp. 24-25 that occurred almost forty years ago. Since that same arrest was reported in earlier editions of this book and records that old could still turn up again, I believe it best to continue reporting it.

This is not the story of my entire life. It is a series of parables selected from my life to present lessons by which you can protect your children from sexual predators. Out of respect for the privacy of others, some locations have been changed and some facts have been omitted. Other than those individuals listed in public records, all names used here are fictional. Because of the subject matter, only analogies of actual sexual conduct have been presented and no graphic depiction of sex with children has been included. Where anyone has been left out of this account it is only because no way could be found to refer to them without making their identity known, at least to some others, and I give myself no right to do that. They may be certain, however, that they will never be forgotten and that, through this telling, others will be spared their pain.

Chapter One

The Making of a Predator

The best suggestion I can give you to protect your children is that you have them help you do so. From the time they can talk, there are steps they can take. This book names many of them. Teach your children these so that both of you are creating a defense together.

Unless things change, it looks as if that is what will be needed. As I've told members of congressional staff now working on new legislation, for the past eight years I have been hearing from convicted sex offenders in prisons across the country. But for the first time in the spring of 2005 I began hearing of death threats to the nation's children being muttered in prison yards. My correspondents warned me that some of the men were saying they were sorry they hadn't killed their child victim last time and that, next time, they would.

It's the sentences: they have gotten too long. Men exposed to them know that, if convicted again, they may never have a chance to come back. '*It's better not to leave any witnesses,*' they're saying.

It's also the country. Since the original edition of this book was published, the nation has made a drastic shift away from bringing sex offenders back to the community after prison. In some fourteen states now, the idea of using Megan's Law to let the neighborhood keep them under control has been abandoned in favor of new laws that forbid them from living in most parts of the cities (anywhere near so-called 'child safety zones' around schools), driving many of them into the countryside.

Some of the men in prison aren't willing to accept this as that means they will have to leave their families behind. "We'll take revenge," they promise.

In response, I've stepped-up my prison outreach project and I've begun going into the prisons to tell the men how they can still earn their way back into the community. I'll be donating copies of the original edition of this book to prison libraries across the nation.

I also decided that I'd better give readers half-again as many ways to protect their children—while telling them two dozen ways they can arm their children to protect themselves—which is the reason for this revised edition. Suggestions based on each chapter appear at its end and all of them appear together at the end of this book. As before, this work's purpose remains that of telling how to keep those you love protected from:

- rapists and child molesters in the streets,
- on the Internet and
- in youth organizations;
- repeated sexual abuse,
- child prostitution,
- incest, and
- repeat sex offenders who move into your neighborhood.

By the time you finish reading the following pages, instead of living in fear for your safety and that of your loved ones, you will know what you and your own neighbors can do to make certain that no sex offender who goes to prison gets out unless he or she has been given the necessary treatment to do so without threatening you.

You will know how sex offenders think and act so that you may tell your children how to keep themselves safe from any who approach them.

And you will know how most sex offenders can be reformed because that's the kind who is writing this book. The U.S. Mint hires former counterfeiters to help catch newer ones. Many banks hire former bank robbers as their security advisors. There is no reason you should do less to protect your child. For what you need to know can only come from someone who has been there.

I was lucky. I went to prison and got help. Now, I'm in my fifteenth year of recovery since coming back to the community and remain re-offense-free. Others could do so, too, but before we get to that it's best to start with how people become predators as you cannot defend yourself against something until you first understand its roots.

To make the reading of this work easier, all sex offenders will be referred to in the masculine gender even though there are both males and females among them.

Formation

My formation as a predator was no different than that of many others. It began on the Pacific Coast Highway near Malibu on a late summer afternoon when I was thirteen years old and looking for a ride home. I'd spent the day at the beach with all the other kids in my junior high school who had suddenly discovered why there were two sexes. Amidst cooling breezes from the sea that tempered the sun's thermonuclear heat, we had spent the day riding the waves, lying in the sun and sampling the first wines of sexual attraction. But at four o'clock the breezes had intensified, telling us like a mother's call that it was time to go home. We reluctantly gathered up our clothes and trudged through the sand back to the nearby highway.

The girls all had parents who drove down to pick them up—or they took the bus back, as did some of the boys. But the more adventurous of the guys sought rides from strangers and I was invited to join them, standing by the roadside in our tight swimming trunks with towels curled around the back of our necks, tanned and boyish-looking, sticking out our thumbs.

It didn't take long for two of us to get a ride, another kid named Billy and me. We thought getting one right away had just been lucky because we didn't know that we had been watched and tracked for several days by sexual predators who used that highway as their hunting grounds. They knew the exact time we'd be going home and exactly where to find us. Some had even exchanged notes with each other.

On this particular day, the first one who saw us pulled his car over like a hawk swooping down to strike at his prey. He was a hairy man, chunky and in his late thirties and when his car stopped he reached over to open the passenger door and we unknowingly got in.

"Whereya goin'?" he asked, as we adjusted ourselves next to him on the front seat. In unison, we replied, "West L.A.," and giggled to ourselves as the car drove off. Since Billy was going to be getting out first, he was sitting on the outside and I sat in the middle. When the man reached across to make sure the door was firmly locked, I noticed that he pressed the side of his hairy arm against my bare chest, as if trying to feel its adolescent smoothness. That seemed *strange*.

His conversation with us, however, was even stranger. All the way home, he talked of nothing but *sex*: how great it is, how much you can get, all the different kinds of things you can do with a girl. He spoke mechanically and stared straight ahead as he talked, as if in a trance. I thought that most of what he said sounded *dumb*.

My friend's stop came up first and he got out, leaving me alone with the man. My stop was another mile down the road and when we got there, instead of pulling over to let me out, he quickly turned at the corner and drove a few hundred feet away from the traffic before he parked the car by the curb and turned off its motor.

He looked over at me and asked, "What's your name?"

"Robert," I replied nervously, for that's what I was called in those days.

He told me his. Then he said, "You know, all that 'stuff' you can do with girls you can also do with guys!"

I didn't understand, but he went on. "Look," he said, leaning toward me now, "I don't mean to frighten you…but I'm a *homosexual*."

I froze in terror. Only recently had I asked my mother what that word meant and she'd said: "*a man who takes little boys up into the mountains, cuts them up and throws away all their pieces.*"

Hearing it now paralyzed me. I couldn't move a muscle, I was so frightened.

He leaned further toward me, then abruptly halted to look around as if trying to see if anyone else was nearby. Something must have made him change his mind, for he backed away as he continued to speak.

"Y'know," he said, slumping against his door panel, "if you'd meet me back down at the corner tonight, we could go over to my place and I could give you a *real* good time. Whadaya say?"

A distant memory came forth of my mother telling me: *"If you ever meet a crazy man, just say 'yes' to him and he won't hurt you."*

I was so frightened that I would have said anything to get out of that car. "Sure," I replied.

A slight smile crossed his lips and all of a sudden I could move again.

He suggested we meet at seven o'clock and I agreed, then got out to walk the rest of the way home. As he drove away, I noticed his license number and quickly memorized it just in case he came after me.

The telephone was ringing as I came through the front door of my house. My parents weren't home yet, so I ran up the hall to answer it.

It was Billy. "Hey!" he asked. "How they hangin'?"

"Fine," I replied. He wanted to know if I was going to the movies that night, with everybody else.

I told him about the man who'd given us a ride and how he'd told me he was a *homosexual.*

"Weren't you scared?" Billy asked in awe.

"Nah," I lied. I told him how I'd gotten rid of the man by pretending to be willing to meet him later.

Billy was impressed and I acted as if there'd been nothing to it. Then we worked out which girl each of us would try for at the movies that night and got off the phone.

But, twenty minutes later, the phone rang again. This time it was Billy's *father.*

"Robert!" he announced. "Billy just told me what happened to you today. You were very lucky to get away from that man. He's a very dangerous person!"

I didn't want to talk about it with Billy's father. "Yessir," I said. But that wasn't to be the end of it, for he went on. "I've just spoken to a police officer I know and he's on his way over to see you."

Shit!

Two detectives from the Los Angeles Police Department arrived at my house. One said he was from "Juvenile" and the other from "Administrative *Vice,*" whatever that was. In answer to their questions, I repeated what had happened that day and when I told them that I had agreed to meet the man back at the corner that evening "just to get away from him," they glanced at each other.

The Juvenile officer spoke first. "Would you be willing to help us, so we can arrest him?"

It was a chance to a hero, so I agreed. *The girls would like that.*

He said that all I'd have to do is go back down to that corner to meet the man. His partner told me that I wouldn't have to get in the car. "Just touch the door—we'll have squad cars hidden in the driveways, all up and down the street. The moment you put your hand on his window, we'll come get him!"

The other officer cautioned me sternly. "But don't get in his car."

I went down there fifteen minutes before I was supposed to, in case the man came by early. But after I'd been there a half hour, I began thinking he might not show up after all. Just as I was wondering if I could leave, he suddenly pulled up.

"Hop in, Bobby."

I saw him inside, smiling at me hungrily.

Within just a few years, I'd be exactly like him.

But it would be another week before I'd be molested. Not by him. I did as the cops said and only touched the door and they came and got him. It was by a bigger kid at school who heard about it. Previously molested himself, he'd now become a predator of other boys. Like many victims, once word got around that a man had come after me, someone else came after me too. By the time he was done with me, I was lost inside myself. I now liked what was being done to me while the world I knew did not.

Before very long, I was doing no more than living on an emotional fault line.

Just like everybody else in my family. Each had their own reasons, but most had no more faith in themselves than an atheist had in God. Now I was like one of them. And our fault line went back a long ways.

Beginnings

According to the family chronicles, it first became active two hundred years ago in the Russian countryside, when my maternal ancestors were living in a small peasant village outside of Kiev. It was on a crisp spring morning after all the men had hiked down into the valley to tend the fields. Only the old, the women and the children were left behind, on a high plateau dotted with the wood and straw huts which served as their homes. Molly was one of the children, a little girl no more than five years old. She and her girlhood friend, Leah, were sitting on the ground, playing with stick-figures they had wrapped in scraps of cloth.

"Mine is the Czar!" Leah announced.

"Mine is his bride," replied Molly.

But the only marriage that day was to be with death, for as the children played, a troop of soldiers from the Czar's army came galloping up into the village—*to persecute the Jews for having killed Christ!*—and the village was suddenly besieged.

Women screamed and ran for their lives as huts were set aflame. Only the children failed to move, paralyzed with shock. As Molly and Leah sat mutely beholding the horror unfolding in front of them, a horse the color of midnight rode past as its rider leaned over and held his sword out like a scythe. Effortlessly, it harvested the tiny head of Molly's playmate, right in front of her.

Little Molly was found after the soldiers had left, frozen into place directly across from her playmate's lifeless body, still lying on its back in a pool of blood. A blanket was quickly thrown over the tiny corpse and relatives gathered up Molly and comforted her as best as they could. There was nothing else to do and the child's life continued from there. Over the next dozen years, she grew up and her parents took her with them when they immigrated to the United States where she soon married a man from a similarly ill-starred family. Ultimately, she became my maternal grandmother and wore a permanently-tragic look which stamped itself on all of us who descended from her.

Or the story may actually have been about *her* grandmother; the family chronicles aren't clear. All I know for certain is that, somewhere back there, the wholeness of life was shattered for my family—like so many others in lands plagued by war and genocidal strife, whose children will also grow up mad to become the madmen of their times.

From then on, our family became filled with those afflicted by suicide, depression and chronic anxiety. They became habituated to seeing themselves as victims of life and, being unconscious of this, I soon unknowingly adopted it as my own identity.

"You were raised to become a walking *time bomb*," my first prison counselor told me, looking over my file. "You could have gone off a number of different ways. It just *happened* that you became a sex offender."

My mother's childhood was an equally-shattered one. She only vaguely remembered her father, and then with great sadness. The *official* version in the family was that he fell down and *hit his head* in New York City after they had all come to America. But, whatever the actual facts, he wound up being committed to a mental hospital for *depression* when he and my mother and her mother reached California. My mother said that she never forgot taking the long trolley ride down from Los Angeles every weekend to visit him inside the state institution.

"He had been such a *strong* man," she lamented. "It hurt *so much* to watch him wither away."

He died in that hospital when she was five years old. Left to be raised by grandparents while her mother went to work in an uncle's clothing store, she was given an often-insensitive upbringing. Her grandmother, while described as sweet, was also intimidated by her gruff fundamentalist husband: an Orthodox Jew who spent all day praying for God's favor with such fervor that one might wonder if he really trusted his Deity to know that he needed it.

One day, while still little, my mother fell down and broke her arm. It was a compound fracture and she recalled how she could clearly see its two shattered ends poking underneath her skin. In shock, she went home and entered her grandfather's study, mutely standing there, with her limp arm hanging from her shoulder like a broken wing.

He abruptly put his prayer book down and rebuked her. "What's the matter with you?" he bellowed. "Can't you see that I am busy, *speaking to the Most High?*"

She was left an emotional pauper. Fearful of men, but always believing herself to need one, she grew up to marry a man who dominated her, probably in revenge for the way he recalled that his oldest sisters had brutally raised him.

The Flaws of Childhood

An inwardly timid man, my father became a lawyer and sought refuge in the field of law hoping thereby, like most lawyers, to control life. Constantly assuring me that our existence was full of absolute rules, the main lesson he taught was that the only way we could keep from being crushed by the world was by somehow gaining support from its fundamentally-unsympathetic Judge.

Afraid of others wherever he went, he could not even find the confidence to cross the street if there was a car coming anywhere nearby, even blocks away. Holding his arms out to his sides, like wings, to restrain both my mother and me, he'd keep looking back and forth repeatedly while cautioning us, "Wait 'til it's past," even if it was a block away. He'd do the same and halt us, even if we were already halfway across the street, causing it to honk angrily at us to *get the hell out of the way!*

Yet, for all his timidity in the outside world, at home he was The Dictator of the Dinner Table, commanding that dinner always be served at 6:00 PM whether anyone was hungry or not. Whenever the evening meal failed to arrive on time, he'd holler at my mother. "*What's the matter with you? Why isn't dinner ready?*"

She'd quickly hovel in to serve him, a hastily-filled plate in her hands. But, afterwards, she always uttered a vicious word or two under her breath—like a curse—as vengeance against anyone she lacked the courage to face directly. When I was just at the dawn of adolescence, she took me aside and told me in hushed tones that I was adopted because they couldn't have any children.

"*It was your father's fault,*" she whispered.

More seismic damage.

Starving for love, my father didn't know how to attract it, so he took it wherever he could. Every wedding anniversary and holiday, he bought my mother the most overly-sentimental greeting card he could find, then read it aloud as he swooned to himself before clasping me to him and covering my face with thick, wet kisses. As she was frigid, I was made into her emotional surrogate.

She despised the human body and its sexual organs in particular. I still remember her scowl when she bathed me and touched mine. Once— when I was no more than four years old—a hearty banana plant unexpectedly grew up in our Southern California front yard, where it promptly sprouted a large bud looking exactly like an uncircumcised penis. Immediately upon discovering it, my mother ordered the gardener to hack the offending member down.

Not long afterwards, I duly imitated her by plunging the third finger of my left hand in between the moving blades of our gardener's lawn mower.

The severed member was sewn back on, but fears of adequate potency remain with me to this very day.

Like her mother before her, she was a chronic worrier, a perpetually shifting sea of self-doubt constantly flooding my island. Amidst such forceful tides, it was impossible for much of a self to congeal within me. If my face wasn't clean-enough, she'd grab a Kleenex and rub its skin hard while loudly anguishing to herself, "What will people think?" Every time that I said I liked something that she didn't like, she'd insist "You don't *really* like that." Every time I said that I thought something that she didn't happen to think, she'd insist "You don't *really* think that." Every time we went to a restaurant and I wanted to order something that she didn't like, she'd insist, "You wouldn't like that."

Early in my childhood, her stare of disapproval at my very dancing to music on the radio froze my body. By the time I was seven years old, she had also gotten me to freeze my feelings.

My father never resisted her when she did these things to me, perhaps because of a similar emotional robbery when growing up in his own family. But as a result of it all, before I entered puberty I no longer had a soul and all the ingredients were there from which a sex offender (or almost any other kind of severely disturbed person) will grow.

They aren't genetic: so far, the Human Genome Project hasn't had any success in finding genes associated with sexual offending. The sexual predator of tomorrow is still a child today, a very disturbed child. His or her care providers are usually insecure, alienated and plagued with emotional breakdowns in their own families. The child's mother doubts herself and her womanhood, covertly wars against her husband and overly-controls her own children. The father is emotionally distant, fearful and dictatorial in his home, unable to accept his wife as his equal.

The child is physically or emotionally abused and comes out insecure and unable to express his or her own feelings. Add *sexual urges* and such a person can become explosive, very possibly a future sex offender.

If you ever meet such a child, *befriend him* and you may save a life from turning in on itself and becoming destructive. If the child tells you that he or she has been physically or sexually abused, report it to police or Child Protective Services. If the child is being neglected, let the child know that he or she is welcome to visit you.

Saving the nation from its next serial killer, rapist or child molester is simple. If you meet a child who is hungry, feed him. If you meet a child who is cold, give him a blanket. If you meet a child who doesn't have a shelter, become one for him. Don't wait until he grows up to become every parent's worst nightmare. Dare to comfort him now and involve your neighbors so that the child has a small community of adult friends who can be turned to for help. It takes a family to grow a child. It takes a community to heal one.

An Incendiary Mixture

As soon as I entered my teens, even my sex life was dominated by my mother. Every morning after I'd been out on a date, she'd interrogate me over breakfast. Whenever I gave in to her inquisition and confessed there'd been an erotic instant, she rewarded me for it on the sly.

"Shame on you!" she would scold, but with a poorly hidden smile to herself as she stirred the scrambled eggs.

Buoyed by the early adolescent pride her responses gave me, I became even more sexually ambitious with my dates so I'd have more to brag about. In the process, I soon took on the mindset of a budding sexual predator.

But, at Age 16, I found out how counterfeit these sexual feelings were when another boy in my class introduced me to a woman I could pay for sex, downtown. The first time I went to her, I wasn't able to complete the act until I began fantasizing about practices I'd carried on with some of the boys at school.

The result was even more emotional confusion, compounded by problems I was now having at home with my father. I'd begun to read widely and began questioning some of his strict ideas. In response, he would explode in rage, angrily getting up from his side of the dinner table to rip his belt off and lash me with it until I cowered under my arms in terror. As soon as I graduated high school, I ran away and joined the Army to run away from my life until I'd had enough time to figure it out.

I didn't get the answers I was looking for, though. When I tried to get counseling about my sexual feelings from an Army psychiatrist, he threatened me with a court-martial if I said anything to suggest I was homosexual, so I dropped the issue. As a result, by the time I returned to civilian life, I came back just as unsure of myself as I'd been when I'd left it.

And that left me as prey for, within a week of beginning college, a sexual predator among the senior students came after me and began to groom me, then train me.

When Christmas vacation approached, he asked if I wanted to go to Tijuana with him, just across the Mexican border. "We can have sex with some boys there. I know a place." I told him I wasn't interested and he said that if I needed any action while he was gone there was a bar off-campus I could use.

"That place is *always* hot!"

I found out he was right soon afterwards and began participating in anonymous homosexual couplings in its shadowy back rooms regularly. But at the start of the next semester this stopped when I met the first coed who really smiled at me. I was so anxious for the heterosexual life she seemed to offer—and all the comforting sense of being like everyone else that seemed to go with it—that she immediately became my only pursuit. By Easter vacation we were lovers and, that Fall, she was pregnant. We quickly married and my parents gave us money to get our own apartment.

My wife gave birth the following year. As I held the baby in my arms at the hospital, I finally felt I was who I was really supposed to be. And so I silently vowed to myself—in keeping with the homophobic views of those times—that I would never again commit another homosexual act.

I stuck with that resolve for several months but, under the strain of middle-of-the-night feedings and a full load of classes, I soon found myself feeling depressed. In an attempt to get away from the grind of my new life, I took the car and drove into Hollywood one day to run some errands. As I waited for a traffic light to change, a theatrically-beautiful young boy who appeared to be in his mid-teens came over and asked if he could have a ride. I said yes without even thinking and, after he got inside, began talking to him about nothing but sex as we drove away: how great it is, how much you can get, all the different things you can do with a girl. I spoke mechanically and stared straight ahead as I talked, as if in a trance.

"You know," I said to him, as we waited for a light to change, "all that stuff you can do with girls you can also do with guys."

He was puzzled, so I offered him five dollars if he would let me have sex with him. He accepted my offer.

I turned right at the next corner and drove us up into the hills where I parked the car and we did it there.

Afterwards, I was filled with loathing toward him, as if it had been his fault instead of my own. I wouldn't even speak to him as we drove back down and, at the first corner we came to, I let him out and drove away. But, the moment he was gone, all my feelings of revulsion turned back on me and I was disgusted with myself for what I had done.

Those feelings didn't last. As I drove back home, replaying the whole episode in my mind, what I remembered most was how the whole thing had felt as if it had taken place all by itself. It was as if I had been *taken over* by something completely outside of myself the very moment I had first encountered that boy—as if something had *possessed* me into seducing him.

Whatever it was, it took me out of this world with an intoxication that was too good not to want again. For the first time since earliest childhood I'd been free from all the sadness I'd been carrying around within me as well as all the anxieties about my future that were now their children. By the time I got back to my apartment what I knew was that, if that seductive force—whatever it was—ever beckoned again, I would *welcome* its embrace and go after another boy.

I was a predator now.

*   *   *

How to Protect Your Children

1. Teach your children not to hitchhike: in cars or on the Internet.
2. Teach them to get away from any adult who starts talking to them about sex.
3. Ask them to tell you who their friends are, and their ages. If they are much older, ask them to see that person only in your home, when you can be around too.
4. Warn them that there are also children who have already been abused who may try to abuse them.

*   *   *

Questions to Consider

1. We say that the child who was molested was a *victim*. Does he remain one if he goes on to molest another child?
2. Does he remain a "victim" even when he is an adult?
3. Where should the line be drawn between 'damage that has just passed through him' to damage that he, alone, is responsible for having created? Is there such a line?

Chapter Two

Theology of Sexuality

Not all of us who are molested as children grow up to become child molesters. Most do not. As almost all of the experts agree, that only happens if the damage has been significant enough and we haven't been given sufficient help afterwards. As I told Oprah, the damage doesn't have to be physical and she agreed with me: the damage is to the spirit. (*The Oprah Winfrey Show*, February 25, 2003.) If the erotic is opened to a child too early, he gets stuck there.

There was a man and he didn't even touch me. All he did was offer to do so in a way that I found so threatening that I couldn't move a muscle. Then a bigger boy came after me like a rapist. Of course my sexuality was affected: those were my first sexual experiences with other people.

There's a model I've come to see repeatedly with child sexual abuse. A child is sexually molested and, if the damage is deep enough and the child is given no help, the damage appears to incubate inside him—for approximately ten years or so—and then reproduces itself in the form of a compulsion that suddenly breaks out—'takes him over'—and causes him to do the same thing that was done to him, on someone else just like he was then.

Just as he had no understanding of why he had been molested in the first place, he now has no understanding of why he has come to abuse someone else. It's as if he's in a spell.

But not afterwards. From then on, he is choosing to be spellbound. He's giving himself to whatever is at the heart of it. You might say that, at this point, he has accepted the invitation.

Searching the Night Seas for Sex

A short time after I had picked up my first teenager I was out of college and working. Each evening when I went home, I had to drive through Hollywood and, en route, there were always a lot of teenage boys hitchhiking. Intoxicated by my recollection of that first incident, seeing these other boys made me want to repeat it. I did so with them whenever I could. As with that first boy, I offered them money for sex and they readily took it: some, because they may have subscribed to the popular American belief that 'money makes anything okay.' Little *ho's*, they call themselves now. Others, just to give themselves an excuse to try something they wanted to do anyhow, out of curiosity.

Not all of them, of course. I had my refusals. But I had more than my share of those who willingly sold themselves out for no more than the cost of a Big Mac.

Having no way of knowing—when I stopped to pick up a boy—whether he would or wouldn't accept my proposition, I quickly noticed that a certain kind of boy was more likely to be susceptible than others: lonely boys, lost and outside of themselves, boys whose self-definition had not yet been formed. Boys who had troubled relationships with their parents. Any boy who admired his father or had self-confidence was never available to me.

Since finding my kind required that I make an accurate assessment of him before I made my offer, I always began psychologically scanning every rider from the first moment he got in my car. It's the same thing that Internet predators are doing today with kids in chat rooms and on blog sites.

I would begin by asking him to tell me about himself, how he got along with his parents, what he liked and what he didn't, whether he'd had any success with girls yet or not. When I had someone who I thought might say yes, I'd bend our conversation further into the subject of sex and casually ask if he had ever thought of experimenting with it "like some people do."

If my prospective victim said that had no appeal to him, I'd quickly agree—"I don't blame you; neither would I"—trying to seem just as normal as anyone else. Then I would quickly make up some excuse to get rid of him so that I could begin hunting for someone else. "Oh! I'm sorry. I forgot I have to stop at a market up-ahead. Let me drop you off here." ("Gotta leave the chat room now to go have dinner.")

But if he said that he was open to the idea, he was mine. That's when the mystery began to descend: that feeling of a net being cast over both of us, drawing us together toward something I couldn't name but which now commanded. Bewitched by the mood, I lost all sense of self and, instead, gave in to my urges and desires.

Psychiatrists tell us that there's a chemical reason for this. Apparently, the more someone becomes sexually excited, the more certain chemicals start to be secreted within the brain. These actually shut down our reasoning faculty, leaving us with nothing else but our sexual urge. Any other mental faculty has been sedated.

Sometimes I didn't find the kind of prey I was looking for, only young adults—and some not so young—in campus restrooms or waiting on some secluded trail in certain public parks. They'd do if my thirst was great enough. If the hour was late, I could always find a male prostitute on Hollywood Boulevard, but I really didn't care much for them—they had no innocence left to consume.

People have asked me how many victims I had, as if that would tell them something significant. But I never kept score, so I don't know and I question whether the answer would mean that much, except to a clinician. Just as a young, normal heterosexual male will have a certain number of successful sexual encounters if he has the looks or skills to attract them, so will a sex offender of the same age: the number won't be any more or any less. What is different about us is not how many times we do it, but who we go after and why. A number of the boys I found may have been gay and were just trying to come out. Others may have been passing through a bisexual stage in their lives, which is very common in adolescence. I was always glad to help them check it out.

We seek kids who aren't sure of themselves yet and lack self-confidence, perhaps because those traits mirror our own. Lost as I still was, it was impossible for me to think of anyone as my *victim* or to think of myself as their *predator*. Instead, it only seemed like a harmless diversion on the way home, *no more than a game* that I was playing to amuse myself. I was so blind that I didn't even see it as cheating on my wife, as no other woman was involved.

People accuse us of being deceptive and we are. We pass ourselves off as if we are like everyone, just so we can get close to our prey and strike. We're your banker or lawyer or service club president. We're your youth group sponsor. Man of the Year. Pillar of the community. Maybe even your priest or minister or rabbi.

What most people don't know are the depths of our deception. Its dark genius lies in the fact that we also deceive ourselves. We think that we're really *quite okay*, no different than anybody else, other than during these little *episodes* of ours. That's why we are able to deceive others. We pose as ordinary people until we believe it too, because facing the real truth about ourselves is so painful. The shame that hovers over us is like an impending avalanche. We fear that if we ever let ourselves see what we really are, so much shame will come crashing down that we will be buried under it, when the truth is that we're already buried under a power we don't yet know how to escape.

So we deny who we are to ourselves and, by so doing, deny who we are to you. Don't blame yourself if we succeed and your child is harmed. How could you have possibly spotted us when we also conceal ourselves to ourselves? Because I could not see how harmed I had become through having been molested, how could I possibly understand that I was harming anyone else?

But, as time went on, I did begin to see something else: that the urge to go hunting for sex was coming upon me more often than before. All by itself it was beginning to increase in frequency until, finally, it was taking me over every ten days and making me play whether I wanted to or not.

That scared me, so I tried not to think about it. But a second self had now taken root within me: my urge for predatory sex had now become a personality as autonomous as my own. It had its own intentions and it didn't care at all about any of mine.

At first, I called it *The Voice*, as it began as an urge that would speak to me, prompting me to consider going after boys at that very moment.

Playfully, I named it "El Vo-say." Later, I would come to more accurately describe it as *my sexual predator.*

Its episodes always began the same way. I'd be living my life just like anyone else and then a pool of sadness would flood my mind. It was like hearing the sobbing of an abandoned child; when his pain became too intense it became my own and I suddenly found myself thinking of *sex* with a boy in his teens, someone with a trim build and good, clean looks—still pretty enough to be a woman. And if he was a little shy, or a little scared…that really turned me on.

Such thoughts smothered my inner pain, just as thinking about booze does for a drunkard.

That is when I would take my car and begin my prowl. It became my exit strategy from a past full of too many hurts that still weren't healed.

Like all serial offenders, I periodically tried to ignore my urges but always failed. They came when they would, like riptides, and whenever I tried to resist them their current just grew stronger.

Sometimes I'd believe I could overcome them, if only I could find more willpower. Those were the times when I'd get close to that tenth day and let myself think: this time I'm going to prevent it.

It's over, I'd tell myself, and drive directly home without stopping to give anyone a ride. But my resolve was never strong enough and the next day the urge would return, even more powerfully: sex would be on my mind all day and I'd barely make it home instead of going off to hunt. Those were the times when I'd believe I had finally won. But, late that night, the urge would always come back to evict me from my marital bed like the tossing and turning of an angry sea—it wouldn't stop until I slipped out of bed, got dressed and snuck outside while my wife slept.

'Just to take a drive,' I'd tell myself. 'Maybe go down to the beach and up the Pacific Coast Highway a bit. *Not for sex*—I don't want to do *that* again—just to relax. I'm under a lot of stress.'

But instead of driving south, as I should have, the moment I reached Hollywood Boulevard the urge would overcome me and I'd swing the car into a hard right to begin trawling the night seas for sexual encounters. And as I trawled I'd begin to imagine what my ideal dream boy would look like, until the picture of him that I formed in my mind became so real that I finally thought he really existed.

He'll be at the next traffic light, waiting for a ride!

And, when he wasn't there: *He'll be in Beverly Hills!*

He'll be down on the Coast Highway!

He'll be out in the Valley!

On through the midnight streets of the city I'd drive, chasing my phantom lover until dawn. Then I'd drive back home, exhausted, under the scolding light of a raw red sun—telling my wife that I'd been out for a drive because *I hadn't been able to sleep last night.*

Internet predators do the same thing when they learn they are communicating with a child: they instantly create a fantasy of what the child will look like, and that is what lures them into seeking a meeting. If they ever realized that all they were chasing was their own imagination, they could enjoy it in the privacy of their bedroom with a sexual lubricant and leave the kids alone.

I could have done the same, but hadn't yet realized that all I was chasing was myself.

When my night voyages were successful, I'd return as satisfied as the captain of a wealthy merchant ship. Until I reached port, for there was always a band of angry harbormasters waiting within me when I got back and I also had to face them.

There was the Unforgiving Customs Officer:

How could you have done this? It's sick. All the psychiatric textbooks say so. What's the matter with you? You're living like 'Jekyll-and-Hyde,' pretending to be so good when, actually, you're just evil!

There was the Master of the Brig:

You'll get caught, you know. It's only a matter of time. One of these days, the police are going to catch you, and when they do they'll put you away forever, like the madman you are!

And finally, the ship's insurance agent:

You'd better be sorry! You'd better get down on your hands and knees and beg for forgiveness, or those forces will carry you away forever and you'll lose everything!

Their roar was my own remorse and it always overcame me. *"I'll never do it again,"* I'd promise myself. *"Never! It will never happen again. I swear it!"*

That would still them and I could walk ashore. But inside myself I knew it would take more than that; what I really needed was professional help if I wanted to stay ashore.

The sad truth, however, was that I really didn't want help yet because I still loved those voyages too much to give them up. Even though I realized I might get caught—and that terrified me—I couldn't stop myself. The sheer dangerousness of what I was doing only heightened my intoxication. I came to like the zest that danger gave, so much that it didn't matter what the penalties might be. At that point, I didn't think there was a law that could deter me. Laws are persuasive only to a rational man, not to one commanded by his urges.

Nor have they any effect on a person who secretly wants to destroy himself. It takes work to run a life responsibly and, if you aren't adult enough to accept that fact, the idea of letting it all get washed away can also sound deliciously liberating.

That's how adrift I was when I encountered my first island of hope.

The Call

It was on a weekend afternoon and I had left my apartment to take a walk. Only a few blocks away I came upon a strange building set back from the street, one that I'd never noticed before even though I'd driven past it each day. It was a white, square structure with an onion-domed top painted gold. Curious, I walked up a path that led around its side where I found it had a stained glass window through which I could see rows of pews inside, and an altar, as if it was a church of some kind. That was when I noticed another building, right behind it: a small, wooden cabin of forest green, with its front door propped open.

Walking over to look within, I discovered it was a small bookstore. When I entered, I was greeted by the scent of sandalwood incense. The sound of music from India was playing softly from somewhere further inside.

Just at that moment, from behind a pair of dark curtains at the far end of the room, a gray-haired woman draped in a light blue robe came out and smiled a greeting when she saw me.

"Welcome," she said, motioning with her long thin arm to a couple of chairs nearby. They sat with a small table in-between them, next to a large white bookshelf. "Won't you join me?" she asked. "I've just made some herbal tea."

Her manner made me feel so at ease that I accepted her invitation and sat down. Pouring two cups of tea, she brought them over and, once seated across from me, I remarked, "You know, it's strange. I drive past this place all the time but I've never noticed it before."

"That's often the case," she replied, as she raised her cup to take a sip.

"Pardon me?"

She set her cup back down and smiled. "Until we're ready, we never see it."

I was inside the bookstore of the Vedanta Society, an organization teaching a universal gospel based upon the beliefs that are at the core of all of the world's great religions. Its temple was the building I had seen outside.

The woman's gentle manner encouraged me to talk, and I soon found myself telling her all about myself: how I'd grown up on the West side of town, once wanted to become an astronomer, the ambitions I held now. She listened with such an easy acceptance that I almost slipped once and told her of my sexual problems, but stopped myself just in time. She caught my discomfort with her smile, then reached for a book on a nearby shelf and pulled it out.

"This is something you should read," she said, offering it to me.

I tried to avoid taking it as I already had plenty of other books to read at home, but she wouldn't be put off and pressed it on me. "It's all about a man like you."

"Me?" I replied, in some embarrassment.

"Yes," she said. "Like you, he was very ambitious man and finally found what he thought would be the greatest opportunity of his life. He was a warrior and was about to participate in what was to become India's greatest battle. How eager he was when he arrived at the field of combat. The moment he saw it in the distance, he commanded his charioteer to take him right up to where the front lines would be formed. It was only when he got there that he found who it was he would really have to fight."

She paused in her telling and, enchanted now, I asked: "Who?"

"Himself," she replied with a gentle smile. "Who else is there to conquer?"

I bought the book and read it that afternoon.

And again that night.

It was entitled *The Song of God: Bhagavad-Gita*, a classic from India, and its lessons are profound. It teaches that each of us has a fate we cannot avoid as we live out a relationship between the ordinary self that is just human, and a far superior Ultimate Self within us which is the representative of an Ultimate Source that creates, maintains and destroys the entire universe.

When the hero of the story discovers that the troops facing him include members of his family—uncles and cousins and nephews—he refuses to go into battle rather than harm them, for he is revolted by the thought of killing his own relatives.

That is when God comes forth and, speaking through the mouth of the hero's charioteer, reminds the hero that killing is his duty as one born to be a warrior. Further, that it will make no difference whether he kills or not: whenever a person is doomed to die, he will, whether by the hand of one man or the hand of another. If it is foreordained, it cannot be avoided.

My mind ricocheted back to that time when I was thirteen years old and how, after having just been saved by the police from a man who had meant to molest me, I was molested by one of the bigger boys from school only a few nights later.

Was that destined to happen, regardless of what had been done to prevent it? Is each of us doomed to be what we are? The book said that our desires are natural, and that we can only achieve perfection by fulfilling our nature.

Did that mean I was to live as a *sex offender*? Was I to give way to my urges and not even attempt to control them? Clearly not, for at the same time the *Gita* says that we must renounce our cravings, control our senses and act without lust—while continuing to act!

How could I do this?

Each of us has a duty, it counsels, ordained by our nature and we are helpless to avoid it. Therefore, it teaches, we *must* act—but without being attached to the fruits of our actions. We are, instead, to do each act as *an offering to God.*

I found that troubling. How could I do as the *Gita* suggests and play the part assigned to me while at the same time avoiding lust, as it also counseled? Night after night, I walked back down to the Vedanta Society's temple and sat on its steps, agonizing within myself in the darkness as I tried to figure out its teaching. I couldn't help but do so, for the *Gita* also promises that, if a man loves God enough, *no matter how foul his nature,* in time his nature will be cleansed.

How I longed for such a result as the years of my captivity continued.

I went back to using that off-campus bar again until I suspected that I was using it too much. The sexual pleasure of my adventures there was getting too intense and I began to fear where it might take me. In a desperate attempt to rescue myself, the next time my urge to go there surfaced, I stopped at a pay phone en route and called up the police, anonymously, and reported the place. "You should close it down!" I said.

"Sorry," the officer said, on the other end. "We've got other priorities."

What the hell, I thought, if they don't care, why should I? And I went back there and continued using it.

A few months later, I stopped by just after noon and I was surprised by how few men were present.

Strange, I thought. But, then, it was the middle of the day and it usually didn't get active until later on.

Looking about in the shadows for a partner, I saw a slightly older man approaching me. He was well over college age and had a cruel look to his face, which I found repellant, and I turned away.

He followed me and I retreated again. When he approached the third time, I turned around to face him and demanded, "Why don't you butt out?"

A look of shock crossed his face. "Butt out? *Butt out?*"

His hand suddenly reached into his back pocket and he pulled out a badge. *"POLICE! You're under arrest!"*

My whole world dropped away. Grabbing me by an arm, he hustled me through a side exit into the blinding light of day where a partner in plain clothes came over from a nearby police car and helped handcuff me and place me in the back seat. I was driven down to the same station I had been taken to as a boy, that night when I'd helped police capture a man who had wanted to molest me. Now I would be booked there as a sex offender myself.

Out on bail later, I returned to court a few days afterwards and, after a humiliating ordeal, paid a fine.

I should have known that this was my wakeup call and that I had to get help. But to do so would have required me to finally face what I had become and I was still too afraid of what I might see. I never went back to that bar, though, and even stopped looking for hitchhikers so constantly.

A call to live another way had just been sounded.

*   *   *

How to Protect Your Children

1. Never leave your child in a youth group that leaves any child alone with one adult instead of two and, preferably, of the opposite gender from each other.

2. If you want your children to feel safe in telling you that they were touched or approached inappropriately, make a sacred promise to yourself not to react in anger or distress or that will keep them from telling you.

3. If you ever have a child who has been sexually molested—or even threatened with being sexually molested—use any of the national referral organizations for abused children listed under the Readers Resources section in the back of this book and take the child to a treatment provider so that there isn't any damage left in them to flow through later.

4. Teach your children that *oral sex* is sex, too.

5. Teach them that oral sex can also give them sexual illnesses.

6. Teach your children that the test to live by isn't how it feels but how they will feel about themselves, afterwards.

*   *   *

Questions to Consider

1. What could a parent or care-provider do to give their children the self-confidence that keeps many child sex predators away?

2. If laws aren't enough to stop the compulsive sex offender, would you favor leniency if he turned himself in? If so, under what terms?

3. Right now, mental health counselors are required by law to report any case of child sex abuse, which keeps many offenders from seeking help from them before they are caught. Should this law be revised?

4. Should members of the clergy be required to report those in confession who admit to molesting a child?

Chapter Three

Victims and Consequences

In the months following my arrest, my wife and I parted and then divorced. I bought a camper van, wandered for a while across the United States and back again, returning to the West Coast where I wandered for the better part of the next ten years or so. I encountered shamanism, the Human Potential Movement, Free Sex, and Zen Buddhism. Strange as it may seem, I also participated in a bisexual orgy scene for a while with girls of college age.

I was never a child molester as much as I liked to get lost in sex. Rather, I took it whenever I could, like the alcoholic who will drink anything that will get him intoxicated. And after I had encountered all of these experiences, I married again in my forties and went down to Los Angeles to go to law school. That's where I met Snap and found out what happened to boys like those I had molested.

It was at a part-time job, over at a counseling center in Hollywood, where I came to clerk for a number of its attorneys who defended gay men and women when they got into trouble. Snap used to hang out in the lobby there, as a lot of the gay kids did, for they had youth services there, too.

In his late teens or early twenties, he had been on The Street, as we called it, since age fourteen: nearby Santa Monica Boulevard, where in-between gay bars and gay bathhouses and a beat that never stopped, teenage male hustlers regularly plied their trade. With chestnut-colored hair and a lean build, he had the hungry animal look of someone who had been on the hunt for a long time. I saw him sitting outside my office one day when I got ready to go on a coffee break. I'd seen him a couple of times before and now he was giving me the 'hi' sign, so I motioned for him to come along. It was at a fast foods restaurant next door that he told me his story.

The One-Hundred Dollar Trick

"I ran away from home when I was just a kid," he said, in between quick gulps of coffee. He'd come from somewhere in the Midwest.

"I got on the highway and stuck out my thumb and the first dude who picked me up was a businessman of some sort, an older guy, like, in his fifties. He offered me ten bucks for sex."

Ten dollars was a lot of money in those days, especially to a runaway kid. "Afterwards," Snap said, taking another quick gulp, "he let me off and drove away and I felt that crisp new ten dollar bill in my pocket and thought, 'I got myself a *career* now!'" Other older men quickly obliged his need for customers and by the time he'd crossed the country he was in the company of a man who lived in L.A. "In Hollywood," Snap said, with excitement. "This dude had a pad high up in the hills, with a swimming pool and a stereo and a color TV that I could watch all I wanted. He was gone all day, so I just smoked dope and got high and it was good."

What about sex?

"Oh, yeah. We had that too. At first he wanted it every night, but I told him, 'Hey, man, I'm just a kid! Take it easy.'" Snap laughed slyly. "He backed off after that."

He took another gulp of coffee.

Since the man had financially supported Snap and now Snap was on The Street, it was pretty obvious their relationship had ended. I was curious to know why he thought it had. Snap lit up a cigarette and took a quick drag. "Aw," he said, exhaling. "He tried to 'father' me—wanted me to go to school, 'make something of myself.' It was the same old crap I'd heard at home, so we finally broke up."

But I'd already heard otherwise from Snap's counselor: the boy's adult companion had gotten his feelings hurt when Snap had told him that he could never be anyone's 'father' as all he wanted to do was have sex with boys, and the man had insisted that he leave.

Snap admitted it when I repeated this. "Yeah," he said, wearing a grin of embarrassment. "But it worked out okay. He called a friend of his and arranged for me to stay there, and this other dude came over and picked me up and I went home with him."

It soon became the same story all over again: sex at first, then a fumbling try by a child molester to become a surrogate father. Quarrels and then an ouster. Snap went to a third man's home and, this time, the man wanted Snap to be a party favor for three of his friends one night and Snap got so scared that he ran away.

He made it down to Hollywood Boulevard, where he tried to panhandle passers-by for enough to eat, but got nothing. Then a tall, thin black kid, just a few years older than Snap, wearing a gold earring and a long fake gold necklace came up to him. He'd been watching and thought Snap was trying to sell himself.

"Chi-al? You ain' never gonna score here. This ain't the place for that kind of action."

When Snap tried to explain, his listener didn't care and quickly tutored him. "Go down to Santa Monica Boulevard. That's where all the trade is, and you trick there. You'll make out fine."

Snap was hungry and did as he was told. That first night he got a man to rent him a motel room that he could stay in after they were done, and enough money for a decent meal at a nearby restaurant.

The following night, Snap went out on The Street again and scored once more. Soon, he met other boys like him who schooled him further. When they heard his story of what had happened with the first man he had lived with, their reactions were automatic. "You should have robbed him!"

Many such boys did, and the files of the West Hollywood Sheriff's Office bulge with complaints from nearby hillside residents who report that they have had their car and jewelry taken by their former *houseboy.*

Snap soon began to pool his nightly earnings with those of the other boy-prostitutes as he joined in their life of fast foods, fast sex, powerful drugs, shared motel rooms and sex with each other whenever they could afford to get high together.

They had dreams. All hustlers on The Street in Hollywood have dreams, always centered around their regular customers—the ones who always come back, at least at first.

"He's gonna take me to Hawaii!"

"He's gonna get me in the movies!"

"He's gonna buy me a car!"

"He once gave me a hundred dollars!"

"Bull shit! No one ever gave you a hundred dollars. You're just a five-dollar-fuck!"

"Fuck you!"

"Fuck *you*!"

Snap became a pro and that's how he did it.

We finished our coffee and I went back to my office. A month later he called me from the county jail.

"I'm in *trouble*, man. Big trouble. I'm scared shitless. You gotta come down here and help me. Please! I think they're going to gang-rape me!"

I got in my car and went down immediately and he told me what had happened.

Among the regular customers on The Street there was a retired businessman from The Valley who came into Hollywood every weekend and rented a room in a Sunset Strip motel where he brought the boys he bought for sex. He'd already had Snap several times in the past and no longer wanted him, for child molesters crave variety. But when he saw Snap coming out of another room, he hailed him over and said, "Look, you go upstairs, to the third floor. There's a dude up there who will pay you one-hundred bucks to have sex with him."

He flashed Snap a fifty-dollar bill and explained. "He paid me this much just to get him a kid. Go do him and the hundred's yours."

Snap was already spaced-out from just having had sex, and he was also high on drugs. His judgment was flawed. All he could think of was finally being able to say that he'd had a one-hundred dollar trick—for that was magic on The Street; it meant that you were extra-special—so he agreed to do what his contact suggested and went upstairs.

When the door opened, he found himself being greeted by a man with dark eyebrows and a menacing look who motioned him in with a flick of his head. The moment the door closed behind Snap, the man bolted it shut. That's when Snap saw two other men emerging from the kitchen on the other side of the room.

And one of them held a whip.

Snap grabbed a nearby table lamp and hurled it at the men, kicked the one in the groin who'd let him in, pulled the bolt and tore the door back open and fled downstairs, furious with the retired businessman for having set him up.

He pounded on the door to the man's room and when it opened he hurled his fist at the man's face. The man ducked, then shoved his way past Snap to run away. Snap chased after him.

The man got into the motel's elevator and its doors closed just before Snap caught up with him.

Snap raced upstairs and when the elevator doors opened, he leaped inside and began to beat the man as the man frantically pressed the down button. The two of them descended together as Snap pummeled the man's face.

Snap was wearing a leather bracelet that night, with stainless steel spikes on it, and they left the man blind.

The beaten man slumped to the floor, unconscious from the pain, and Snap dug into the man's pockets and grabbed his car keys. When the elevator reached the ground floor, Snap jumped out, raced over to the man's car and drove it away. For the rest of that night, he drove in huge meaningless circles all over Hollywood, not certain where he was going or what he should do. At dawn, he returned the car to the motel where police were waiting. Now, he was in the adult section of Los Angeles County Jail and he was afraid that he was going to be gang-raped.

"Please!" he begged me, speaking into a telephone from his side of the thick glass window in the Visitors Room. "Get me out of here!"

He looked quickly to his left and right and then leaned forward as he said into the telephone, *"I'm not really an adult. I'm only seventeen!"*

The moment I told the deputies that, three of them took him away. He was driven right over to a juvenile facility and placed there until his court appearance.

We all thought. But five days later, I received a call from a lady who worked at the juvenile detention facility, an older woman who had labored in Juvenile Hall for years and knew all about kids.

"He ain't no *ju*-venile," she said. "His face-hair growin' back too fast foh ah *ju*-venile. You bettah come on down here."

I did, and Snap confessed that he was really nineteen.

I called his Public Defender and was told to meet him in court that afternoon, where a judge appointed me to assist the court by getting in contact with Snap's family to verify his correct age. They let me talk to Snap and he gave me an address for some relatives who lived way out at the northernmost end of Los Angeles, in the San Fernando Valley. I drove out there that night, only to find that the street he gave me ended in the surrounding desert before it had a number even remotely like the one he had supplied. Snap had conned the system.

And the court wasn't having any more of it. He wound up being tried as an adult and was given six years and sent to San Quentin.

If he survived it.

Our law says that a child lacks the capacity to consent and cannot agree to engage in sex. Scientific evidence supports this concept. According to a bulletin published by the American Bar Association in 2003, the ability to understand what the long-range consequences may be to any activity is an ability that the human brain does not have in full until a person is in their early twenties. The brain isn't fully formed until then and that leaves the child unable to be an equal partner with any adult until that time.

It's not hard to see what came to Snap from living in the world of the runaway. That kind of life can erase any other. And maybe life itself.

Sex isn't just a recreational drug. It's a psychological power. Primitive peoples understood this and worshipped it as a goddess, treating it with reverence.

Increasingly, our culture does not and the results speak for themselves. As I would soon learn, there are consequences for living that way and they are harsh.

For sex can also be tragic.

Something Coming Down the Street: Incest

Law school began late that summer. It was to be an intensive, two-year program, requiring full-time attention by all of its students. But I wouldn't let my connection with the counseling center go. It was too exciting—the pulse of the place, its nonstop phone calls, lawsuits and trials all the time, lawyers from all over the country asking us for advice. And so was the lifestyle that I found with it. *The sex. The drugs. The Boys.*

The Street.

Lectures began late that summer and homework assignments were given out daily: reading and analyzing key cases in various fields of law. On my first exams I couldn't seem to give my professors what they wanted and my initial grades were not good ones.

That fall I transferred out of the intensive program and into the more traditional four-year-long one, given at night. I thought that perhaps if I went slower I'd do better. But my home life made that impossible. My new wife and I fell into a love-hate relationship almost from the beginning and, like many mutually-injuring couples, all we were doing now was keeping score. We tried to break up, but an early pregnancy brought us back together for another try.

It didn't work and as my efforts—both at the Center with its attorneys, and in law school—consumed more of my time, my new wife seemed to become more and more alienated from me. We started to take Lamaze birth training together, but our continuous quarreling kept us from completing it.

A month after our daughter was born, my wife took the child with her and left me for the Christmas holidays. When she returned, our marriage began its final phase of disintegration. A couple of years later it ended when my wife left me for another man and filed for divorce.

Even then, I remained willing to do anything to win her back if only because our marriage had allowed me to maintain my lifelong fiction that I really was as normal as anyone else. The result was that, when our divorce proceeded and she offered me a shared custody arrangement under which our daughter would live part of each week with her and part of each week with me—creating regular times when my wife and I would see each other as the child was exchanged between us—*times when I might win my wife back!*—I eagerly agreed.

Such hopes turned out to be an illusion, however, as my wife had no interest in coming back now. Over the next couple of years, she grew even more distant and the amount of time that our daughter was staying with me increased each week until, by the end, she was living with me all week long and with her mother only on weekends.

I came to feel "trapped" into taking care of our child and wallowed in self-pity. I lost all my self-confidence. I no longer considered myself attractive. I felt rejected as, over and over again, my ex-wife came to drop our daughter off or pick her up and remained deaf to my pleas to stay. She was working as a cocktail waitress at a glamorous nightspot up on the Sunset Strip and every time she came over she was dressed like a million dollars. And every time she turned me down and left, it was like being rejected all over again.

I began to drink more than before. I began using recreational drugs more than before. Isolated and without friends, I soon became desperately lonely.

My daughter increasingly filled that loneliness until I found her to be more a source of love than my ex-wife. Like countless men before me, and countless men to come, that is when I began to look to my daughter for the kind of emotional relationship I could no longer have with her mother.

It wasn't long before I crossed the forbidden line. The same destructive urges as before—that had ruled the rest of my life—returned and, once again, took what I loved the most.

But don't let my pathos deceive you. Incest isn't a crime of sex, it's a crime of anger against the other parent. In a rage that is blinding, the parent fails to see how much harm he is bringing to the child and, instead, does the one thing still left to send the other parent a message that says, "I hate you just as much as you hate me."

Incest is not just a crime, it is also an illness. To treat it solely as a crime is only to injure the child further.

Called to Answer

In September of 1985 I had only recently received my law degree and moved into a new apartment in West Hollywood. I was working on a mayhem trial in the superior court involving a defendant who had injured her husband during a family altercation. As the hearing progressed, the deputy district attorney on the case and I came to respect each other's work. Therefore, when I got the court's permission to go to the women's prison to see if it had any of the counseling programs I insisted the defendant needed, my opponent asked to come along and I welcomed her doing so. We drove out together, spending the day there. Upon our return to Los Angeles, I dropped her off at her downtown office and returned to my new residence, only to learn from messages left on my answering machine that my father had passed away that day.

Shaken, I called the D.A. up and told her. She was immediately sympathetic and that helped stabilize me. I phoned my ex-wife and asked her to take our child a day earlier, as I would be involved in helping my mother prepare for the funeral. We agreed to meet afterwards, at my mother's house that Sunday, when the child would be returned to me.

My ex-wife arrived on Sunday as promised, but immediately urged me to speak with her in private for a moment, while our child waited in another room. She was shaken and I could see it. Once behind closed doors, she told me that our daughter had accused me of having molested her.

Although she would later insist—while acting as a witness for the prosecution—that I didn't confirm it until after she'd argued with me, I recall admitting it immediately. "Thank God it's out," I said. For now I could expel it and seek professional help as all my fears of getting caught had just been realized.

It's easy to fault such a person for not having sought professional help earlier, even if imprisonment is what they risk by doing so. But that is asking for a degree of courage from someone who is already so lost that it is almost impossible for them to find it. The result is that the child continues to suffer as their victim. Under a law that only seeks social vengeance, it is the child victims who are punished more than anyone else.

My ex-wife quickly told me she'd already seen an attorney and had the child's accusations reported to the police. "They're looking for you now."

"Better call in our daughter," I said. For, after having worked on cases just like this one, I knew that I might never see her again and I didn't want her left with any unnecessary guilt if that happened.

When she was escorted into the room I told her that she had done the right thing in telling, and that she should never forget it. "I'll always love you," I assured her. We hugged, I said it again, and then the two of them went home and I returned to my apartment. The next day, I called that deputy district attorney with whom I'd been working on that trial and asked her to meet me after work. "It's personal," I said. "And you're going to hear about it through the system, so I'd rather you heard it from me first."

We met at a small restaurant near her office and I told her what had happened with my ex-wife the night before. I couldn't complete the telling before I broke down in tears, and so did she. A moment later, when I tried to go on, she stopped me. "Don't say anymore," she cautioned me, clutching a handkerchief now. "I'm still a prosecutor. Have you got a lawyer?"

"No," I replied. "Can you recommend one?"

A former colleague, now in private practice, was suggested and the next day I called and asked that attorney to arrange for my surrender.

Several days later, my lawyer and I went to police headquarters and I was booked and then released on bail. My ex-wife and daughter were also there, and I told my ex-wife to contact the court and choose a therapist for our child from its list of approved specialists. "I will pay for it," I said and when I went to court I entered a plea of guilty. In return, the court delayed my sentencing hearing for almost a year so my daughter's therapist could have all the time he needed to take care of her, while I got a therapist of my own to work with me.

It is a good thing that I had disclosed my misconduct to that deputy D.A. or I might later have been tempted to beat the case. When the police interviewed my daughter she told them that a babysitter had *also* molested her, and it would have been easy to have some attorney put her on the stand and get her so confused as to which of us did what that I probably would have walked. She was only five years old.

But what would that have done to her? What could I have gained, had I tried to save myself by falsely calling her a liar?

I've never regretted my decision to tell the truth and I urge anybody in a similar situation to do the same thing. It's called an act of decency and it may be your first, so try it on and see if it doesn't feel better than the kind you've been performing.

In any case of sexual abuse within the family—even by a person who comes to act as a surrogate member of the family—the heart of the crime is that it isn't at all like abuse caused by a stranger. Rather, the perpetrator here has taken on some very cherished role in the child's life and, almost always, it's one they tried to perform. In addition to molesting the child, an in-family perpetrator probably also fed the child, housed the child, got medicine for the child when ill, maybe took the child to doctors and dentists and even attended school plays.

The molester developed an *emotional bond* with the child, whether misused or not. Like my situation with my daughter, it may not have been a healthy bond. The molester may, like me, have believed that they loved the child. But to say—as some prosecutors have—that the perpetrator in a family situation "only" meant to take advantage of the child is to damage the child even more. There is rarely, if ever, sufficient evidence to suggest that the perpetrator was only seeking a relationship in which he could molest the child. Rather, the relationship starts as a good one and only gradually decays as the perpetrator's self-control slips away. Depravity is not just a jump—it's an ever-descending journey.

Like it or not—and this is tough stuff—the child in a family sexual abuse situation has just had his or her first sexual relationship, and to cheapen it even more, *as improper as it was for the adult to have created it*, is to tell the child that they aren't worthy of receiving love, and that should be a crime too.

The defendant's misdeeds are evidence enough to convict. It isn't necessary to crucify the child as well and no parent should permit that to be done. The child has just lost a friend because that friendship was defective. They shouldn't lose the other parent's support too. Rather, the child should be comforted in their sorrow for a love that's been lost, *even if should have been,* for their sorrow is real and they need their other parent as their friend while they grieve for that loss.

When the child's grief is past, they can be helped in understanding that they deserved a better love than they got this time, and be assured that they will get one in the future because they deserve it. Until then, they shouldn't be allowed to stop believing in themselves because they've just lost someone else. For if they lose faith in them self, they will lose faith in their life and never let them self have the really fine life that they deserve.

That's the support I hoped her therapist was giving her, while I also did what I could for myself. Hoping to avoid a sentence of imprisonment, I did what almost all people do in cases like mine, and enrolled myself in a sex offender therapy group so that its doctor might testify in favor of my being left in his care instead of being sent to prison. Each week I attended meetings with others just like me at his office, which were enormously painful as, previously, I had been the one to send men to groups like this in my alternative sentencing practice.

I also worked with my daughter's doctor, telling him whatever he wanted to know so that he could help her deal with everything that was going on in her life now. This, too, was enormously painful for me as I was so ashamed of what I'd let myself become.

It was painful for my child too, as now she missed me.

Because of this, the doctor felt that I should continue to see her, but only with a court-approved monitor present—and I did so whenever visits were scheduled. But no matter how hard the monitor tried to stay in the background on those occasions, their being there at all couldn't help but make them very awkward events.

I'm sure it was difficult for them, too.

As the months went by, visits began to be scheduled by the doctor less and less frequently as he let the bonds lessen between my daughter and me, while building new ones between her and her mother.

My sentencing practice vanished within a week of my arrest, and in the sudden vacuum of each day I began to feel a sense of dread, as if 'something' I couldn't exactly picture was coming down my street for me, rolling my whole life up before it.

A lawyer I knew warned me that I was *not* going to get probation. "They're going to *crucify* you!" he said. "You worked for the courts. You know the rule: if you're part of The System and mess-up, they make an example of you. They're going to send you to prison and you may not survive it."

Fearful that he might be right, I began thinking of suicide. A short time later, under the strain, my appendix burst and I was hospitalized.

After I recovered from surgery and got back to my apartment, I began taking long walks around my neighborhood and started to mourn the fact that, up until then, I hadn't taken the time to appreciate any of life's most ordinary things, like the changing of the seasons or the sunset every evening. Would it be too late now, I asked myself, to begin living that kind of life?

A Flash at Dawn

I came upon a non-sectarian meditation group in a house nearby, led by an anonymous man with an anonymous past. He had the bright blonde hair of a Scandinavian and always wore a white shirt and white slacks when he conducted its meetings. In his early thirties and with a slim build, he had an accent I couldn't place. Some said he came from one country, some said he came from another. Speaking to a congregation mostly made up of recovering drug addicts and others one could only call the 'walking wounded of life,' he said that even when your life is smashed you still have a choice: "to be but a broken piece of a master, or a master piece."

There was always a special reserve about him, as if he was only one step in the world.

I began attending his meditation group weekly and then an auxiliary one that his followers held without him on a second night. When it was announced that there would be a weekend-long session, with a private audience with him for all who attended, I eagerly signed up believing that, perhaps, he had the ability to summon some sort of supernatural intervention that might save me from being imprisoned. Given no more than a Sunday School version of religion, that's all I had now to fall back on, when what I really needed was on the graduate level.

On the last afternoon of that weekend, several of his followers took me in to see him alone. He was in a small room, seated on a high-backed rattan chair. In front of him on the floor, there was a cushion for me to use. I sat down upon it and looked up at him. He stared down at me and in a loud whisper asked, "What do you want?"

All of my plans to seek his help through asking for some sort of miracle suddenly vanished and in their place a spontaneous declaration burst forth from my lips.

"To return to the heart of God and never leave it again."

It was a plea for refuge and, a month later, when I was finally in front of my judge to be sentenced, it was granted *but not the way I would have expected.*

The hearing itself took several weeks before it could be concluded, for the courts at that time were so overcrowded with cases to be heard that they had to hear them all piecemeal. Some had time deadlines by which they had to be heard or thrown out and others, like mine, did not. The result was that the cases with deadlines got most of the court's time each day and cases like mine only got a half-hour or an hour, early in the morning.

A further result was that, instead of being concluded after having had no more than four or five full days of hearing at the most, it was stretched out over almost that many weeks. At one point I seriously began to wonder if I would ever be sentenced, or just spend years in legal limbo, coming before the court for a sentencing that might never take place.

That was an illusion, of course. But by the time my case had been fully presented, it kept me from realizing that my sentence was just about to be decided as I thought there might still be another week or so to go. As a result, when I left the courtroom on Friday, I merely looked forward to the weekend and gave no thought about what might happen when I returned to court the following Monday.

I should have for, on Saturday, my attorney phoned me at home.

"I don't mean to sound too pessimistic," he cautioned. "But if I were you, I'd use this weekend to pack up your things—you know, just in case things don't go our way on Monday."

"Sure," I replied. But I wasn't really worried. One of the advantages of being in a state of denial is that you don't worry about *anything*, even if you should. That is also, of course, its major disadvantage. But I thought it wouldn't do any harm to go through my apartment and tidy it up a bit, throwing out stuff I no longer needed, and putting a few things in boxes.

That evening, I went out as usual and had a very nice dinner with a young man I met at a restaurant and bar known to have young men like him available to men like me. We went home afterwards, had sex, slept together overnight and had a nice brunch on the outside terrace of a Santa Monica Boulevard eatery the following Sunday morning. When we parted, I slipped a very liberal payment inside the top of his partly-opened shirt, he smiled and we agreed to get back in touch in a few days to make plans for the following weekend. As far as I could see, there was really nothing to worry about.

I was in *complete* denial. But something deeper inside me knew better and, that Sunday night—or, more accurately, at dawn on Monday morning, only hours before I would be returning to court—I had a dream:

It was dark out on the desert and the sands softly rippled away in front of me. Up ahead, I could just barely make out the figure of a woman shrouded in a dark robe from head to foot, seated on top of a boulder. In her arms she cradled a young man who was unconscious and wearing only a white loincloth. All about us the silence was total.

Suddenly, from the horizon far in back of her, there was a silent burst of white light—like the kind I'd seen as a kid on my newspaper route early in the morning, when they were still testing atomic bombs in Nevada, 500 miles away. It quickly expanded, like a balloon, then deflated and the darkness returned. Immediately afterwards, and directly overhead, I heard a man's deep voice call out of the darkness:

"HOLOCAUST!"

I bolted awake in my bed. It was just before dawn and I was alone.

What kind of a dream was that?

I threw back the sheets, stepped into my slippers and grabbed my bathrobe hanging on the bedpost. Quickly plunging my arms into its long sleeves before lashing it around myself, I walked into the adjoining bathroom. Hot water full of bubbles immediately soaked the thick cotton washcloth and I pressed it against my face to melt away the crust of sleep.

I brushed my teeth, then made my way toward the kitchen to brew a cup of coffee. *Cigarette!*

I walked into the living room that had also served as the office of my paralegal practice. A dark mahogany desk and leather-upholstered chair sat there and I grabbed the pack I'd left next to my wooden in-box the night before. A flick of a nearby lighter and I was sucking in all the assurance I needed.

The dream: *Holocaust!*

While I hardly thought of myself as a practicing Jew in those days, *holocaust* was still a buzz word, one that always caused shadows to quickly flicker past in my mind—of dim memories from earliest childhood, when relatives spoke among themselves in hushed tones in another room, after making certain I wasn't about—of other relatives, still in Europe, who had disappeared…*in all the ashes.*

What could it mean? Why should I have had such a dream, especially today, when I had to go back into court to see what the judge was going to do with me?

My eyes wandered over to a nearby bookcase and that's when I saw a celebrated fortune-telling book from ancient China that I'd bought years before: *The I Ching or Book of Changes.*

I'd tried to use it when I first got it, but it had never worked for me. Perhaps now, I thought, it might tell me what that dream meant, and whether it had anything to do with what was going to happen in court today.

Hurriedly, I got up and brought the book over to my desk and went through the brief ritual it required: of casting three coins six times to seek its answer, writing down how many heads and tails I got each time. When they were totaled, a chart inside the book led me to the page that would give me my answer. Christians have long been known to do the same thing, by holding an important question in their mind while opening The

Bible at random. The first verse they see is said to be their answer. Now, I quickly looked to read mine.

"Bound with cords and ropes, shut in between thorn-hedged prison walls: for three years one does not find the way. Misfortune."

"Bull-shit!" I said to myself, slamming the book shut. "I'm not going to believe that!"

I got up from my desk and went to shave, shower and dress before leaving for court. I was a modern man, and I wasn't about to accept such foolish superstitions!

The courtroom was almost empty when I arrived. Several court-watchers sat in back and I took a seat at the defense table, up in front. All of my character witnesses—neighbors, a couple of colleagues from my work, members of my family—had already appeared on my behalf and now were gone. When my attorney came in, I felt terribly alone.

The judge entered and we all stood up. He was a large, beefy man with a ruddy complexion and there was a very stern expression on his face today. Things didn't look good: only the prosecutor was smiling.

The judge tapped his gavel lightly and said, with mock weariness: "I suppose we'll have the standard plea for mercy now."

My attorney stood up and answered, "Yes, your honor."

"Proceed."

But, halfway through my lawyer's argument that I be spared imprisonment, the judge halted it. "I've heard enough. He's going to prison. Today!"

I had been sentenced both above and below and was taken away as a convicted sex offender. The only question left was whether I would come back as one.

Or come back at all. The judge wasn't so certain. As the bailiffs handcuffed me and led me out of the courtroom, I heard him say to my ex-wife that it might be better if she told my daughter that her father was dead.

    *   *   *

How to Protect Your Children

1. While every incest case is different in some ways, there are certain characteristics many of them have in common: a dysfunctional marriage, a future offender who is sexually insecure, and a child who comes to be used as an emotional surrogate by one of the partners for the other. If you see such a marriage in your family, urge its members to immediately get professional counseling and restore it to health, or completely end it so the child doesn't become its next casualty.

2. If you want parents already trapped in incest to be able to get professional help, so the child can be saved from further harm as soon as possible, tell your legislators that you want the law changed so that no parent who comes to a professional treatment provider for help after the first time they lose control is given a prison sentence. The offending parent should be moved out of the home and placed on probation with regular exams by a lie detector and visits with their child only when a monitor is present.

3. You can put a stop to child prostitution. *Children of the Night* is a private, non-profit, tax-exempt organization founded in 1979 to rescue children from street prostitution. With a nationwide, toll-free 24-hour hotline, a group home, placement in foster homes, drug programs, mental health programs, special education programs and jobs with independent living—all supported by private donations—the organization claims an 80% success rate in getting kids out of prostitution and keeping them free from going back to the streets. Working with what it calls "a small but committed group of detectives, FBI agents and prosecutors" across the country on the "child prostitution circuit," *Children of the Night* prosecutes the pimps who exploit such children while helping to locate missing children and get them returned to their families.

   For further information, go to their website at
   http://childrenofthenight.org
   Or phone the organization at its national hotline: 1-800-551-1300.

If you live outside the United States, phone the police and ask them who is doing the same kind of work there and help them.

The danger, otherwise, could reach you: if you don't stop child prostitution, some of its members may approach a child in your family and entice them "to make a few quick dollars." Child prostitutes can also become accomplices to child sex predators that way, and you don't have to permit your child to become one of their victims.

*   *   *

Questions to Consider

1. What should the neighborhood do when it sees a young boy or girl suddenly living with an adult who doesn't look like their relative?

2. What responsibility, if any, should motels and hotels have when an adult suddenly returns to his or her rented room with an underage child?

3. What kind of person employed as a school teacher is likely to engage in sexual misconduct with a student? What kind of signals should you be watching or listening for?

4. What help could you give to the incest victim, if one were known to you in your neighborhood (or family)?

5. What help could you give to the child's non-offending parent? To the offending parent?

Chapter Four

The Man With Nothing Left to Lose

I'd been given a chance to escape. Just after the judge had said he was going to send me to prison—but not yet for how long—he received a signal from his courtroom reporter. Her shorthand typing machine was running out of tape and the judge called a five-minute recess for her to refill it. I walked outside of the courtroom and stood in the hallway. Almost directly across from me, the door to the building's stairwell was wide open, with its bright "EXIT" sign tempting me.

I'd worked in that building for several years now and knew that all I'd have to do was go through that doorway, take the steps down to the first floor, walk briskly through the lobby and get across the street to where my car was parked. And then I could go…

…where?

My mind flashed back to those times during law school when a criminal attorney called to tell me he had a client who was now a fugitive and wanted to turn himself in. Usually, it was a man who had been on probation or parole, or on bail awaiting trial, and bolted rather than face it. All I had to do was meet the man somewhere and drive him down to the criminal courthouse, where I'd walk him in to the appropriate court after first having telephoned its bailiff to let him know we were coming.

It was a simple procedure. Once in court, a deputy public defender would be summoned to stand with the man while the judge set a date for a formal hearing *and then released the man until that time.*

Why not? Obviously, he wasn't going to run, for he had just turned himself in.

But on those drives down to the courthouse with such men, I'd heard their stories of what living like a fugitive had been like.

You can never stay in one place too long. You use a different name wherever you go. You can't use your Social Security number, so you work under-the-table at whatever they'll pay you. You can't trust anybody. You're always looking over your shoulder to see if anyone's following you. When you go to sleep at night, you always worry about that midnight knock on your door. So, you can't settle down. You can't fall in love with anyone. You can't build any kind of a life. All you can do is stay lonely.

It's the loneliness that finally causes so many to turn themselves back in. That's why I knew that, if I tried to escape, I would just become lost in that loneliness. So instead of stepping toward that Exit doorway, I took a step back from it, leaving me only one place to go—state prison.

It's a good thing I made that choice for, just at that moment, I felt someone's eyes on me, up the hallway, and I turned to look. It was the prosecutor. He was watching me. *He'd been watching me the whole time.*

The Rite of Expulsion

The bailiff came out and told everyone that court was ready to resume. I walked back in and was sentenced, followed by the soft grip behind me of a man's hand on one of my wrists and then the quick cold embrace of a handcuff: first on one wrist and then on the other.

All the insignia of social membership were stripped away from me. My belt was taken off, my shoelaces removed, my pockets emptied. When my car keys were spilled onto the table in front of me, my attorney said, "I'll call your family and have them come get your car."

My lease would soon be terminated for non-payment of rent, my furniture and personal effects removed from the premises, my utility bills left to lapse, my credit cards cancelled, mail would pile up in my mail box until it was full, by which time the postal delivery person would have heard from the apartment house manager that "He was put in prison! His family told me when they came over to remove his goods!" My telephone line would be disconnected, my checking account closed for lack of activity. My safe deposit box would be opened by the bank when it next became unpaid and my valuables kept somewhere and, when not claimed, vanish.

Within just a few months no entry would be left in any record in the city to suggest that I existed. Even the courthouse would ship its records out. I had been banished from the everyday world and it would no longer know of me. I would be taken, instead, to another world, whose entrance is concealed carefully by a paneled door in the wall of the courtroom, which opens to admit the newly-convicted to a flight of stairs he takes down to find that he is now in another building held *inside* of this one.

This inner building is the jail in the criminal courthouse to which all convicted persons are funneled from similar doorways in each of the courtrooms on several floors, and it has its own hallways, lavatories, control booths with deputy sheriffs in them and, of course, jail cells. It's an entire world of its own *under* the courts. An underworld.

At the bottom of the stairs, there was a glass-enclosed booth with some officers inside. One of them spoke to me through a loudspeaker.

"Turn to your right, keep walking until you come to a door, and then halt until the door is opened. Then go inside and keep to yourself!"

I did as he directed and walked thirty steps until I came to a door that was electronically unlatched and then opened. When I stared inside, I saw forty or fifty men, all dressed in county jail dark blue jumpsuits, sitting on rows of flat wooden benches or standing around, looking back at me as my civilian clothes told them I'd just been sentenced. To one side, there was a Deputy Sheriff.

"Enter!"

I walked in and he stopped me and removed my handcuffs, then directed me to take a seat.

I felt too low to even sit on a bench, so I chose the floor next to the end of one, in a corner. I just wanted to die.

A young Latino, with a big mound of dark wavy hair, was sitting on the edge of the bench and looked down at me.

"Hey, Man! How much time they give ya?"

I stared back up and glumly replied. "Ten years."

"Man!" he exclaimed. "That ain't nothin'. You're a well-dressed dude, educated. I can see that. When you get to prison, they gonna give you one of those desk-jobs and you'll cut your time to half that."

That was the law in my state then: "Day-for-Day," they called it. For each day that you worked, they removed two days from your sentence instead of just the one you served.

"You ain't gonna do no more than five years!"

It might as well have been five centuries.

I took out my pack of cigarettes—they were imported ones—and, instantly, a beehive of men gathered in front of me asking for one. As I didn't know if it would be safe to say 'no,' I let them pass the pack around and it was quickly emptied.

I wouldn't be smoking any more imported cigarettes for a while.

Time crawled in that room. When the electronic door opened again, a metal cart with a large cardboard box on top, full of sack lunches, was wheeled in and the sacks were passed around. I was given a cheese sandwich and wearily took a bite.

I looked up at the Latino kid after I'd swallowed the first bite and said, "Tastes like plastic."

He laughed to himself. "They make it that way on purpose so you can shit easier."

I hadn't thought of that.

Later in the day our deputy sheriff told us all to get up. We were taken back into the outside corridor until we came to a large freight elevator where other deputies waited to take us further down in small groups to the building's basement where a big black and white Sheriff's bus awaited, with bars on each of its windows. Its front door was opened to receive us.

"Inside!" a deputy barked.

When we were all on board and seated, the bus drove us up a concrete ramp where other deputies opened a large metal gate to let the bus go into the street. In just a few blocks we came to another driveway with another large open gate that closed behind us, and then the bus stopped.

We were at the main county jail where we were quickly unloaded and herded through a nearby doorway into a large room with jail bars at its far end. A half-dozen large, muscular deputies holding billy clubs waited for us. One of the deputies spoke.

"Form a couple of lines!"

We automatically did so and I found a place in the front row. The deputy spoke again.

"Drop 'em!"

All around me the other prisoners began undoing their jail house jump suits and letting them fall to their feet, so I began taking off my clothes. When I got to my underwear, I looked about and saw men shedding their trunks as well and I did the same.

"All right!" said the deputy. "Turn around."

We did so and had our backs facing him. The other deputies came up behind us.

"Bend over!"

We did so.

"Spread 'em!"

The deputies were checking to make sure that no one had brought back any drugs or money from the courthouse.

We were sprayed for lice, showered with cold water, given a towel and marched back out to stand in line again, next to our clothes heaped on the floor. We put them back on.

"Alright!" boomed the deputy. "Lissen up! Those jail bars behind me are going to open in a moment and you all know where to go. Anyone new, go with them unless you got a 'problem' of some kind."

That was a cue word I had learned about over at the Counseling Center. The Los Angeles County Jail is one of the most violent places on earth. It holds more prisoners than most penitentiaries, and if you don't want to get hurt you do whatever you have to in order to get protective housing in special units segregated away from the main population. Telling the deputies that you are gay is one way to do so and when all the others had left that's exactly what I did. A deputy ordered me to follow him over to a laundry room where my clothes were exchanged for a sky blue jump suit and paper slippers. I quickly changed into them and was then taken outside and put into a small sheriff's van which drove me over to the nearby Hall of Justice, where the Gay Tank—as it was called—was located, high above the streets of downtown Los Angeles.

The Man with Nothing Left to Lose

The Gay Tank had three floors of cells: Pretty Boy Row, where the good-looking kids were kept so they didn't get raped, Queen's Row, where all of the transvestites were housed, and Stud Row for more aggressive homosexuals. Each row was kept segregated from the others to keep the aggressive men from getting to the boys, and the Queens from getting to either. Since I was neither pretty nor queen, I was sent to Stud Row. That's where I would be kept until there were enough other new arrivals to ship all of us on a sheriff's bus to the state prison intake facility a couple of hours away.

An officer escorted me to a very wide corridor split into two smaller ones by a wall of jail bars running down its middle. On one side, that made it into a long hallway, through which inmates marched on their way to chow or Sick Call or the Visiting Room. There were a few windows in the wall on that side, where we could look down to the street below and see tiny cars and ant-sized people walking about in the world that had once been ours.

On the other side of the bars, the corridor was filled by a narrow walkway and, next to it, row after row of very compact two-man jail cells. They were old and each was lit by a single bulb on the ceiling if there was a working fixture there. Within the cell, it was narrow and cramped with one bunk on top of the other, taking up half the space. In the other half, a small washbasin sat next to a metal toilet in the back corner.

My cell was a dark one, my cellmate was in his late twenties, with a pale complexion from having been locked up here too long, and he sexually assaulted me that night, then insisted the next morning that he'd never do that again unless I paid him to, as if the whole thing had been my doing. What I wouldn't realize until I'd been through therapy and seen it in myself is that he didn't know what had driven him the night before—a blind compulsion and not a reasoned choice. Until the courts understand that is what dominates us, they will continue to sentence us like all others who break the law and we'll keep right on re-offending. Other criminals *choose* to break the law. We don't. We break the law more like a sleepwalker would. Or an addict.

But my cellmate was certainly more awake than I when I asked him what he was in here for. "Don't ask anyone that question," he shot back. First, he said, it was none of my business; second, it didn't matter.

"We're all in here for the same reason," he went on. "We got caught, and who you were before isn't important. It's who you are now that counts, because that's who we have to live with.

"Besides," he added, "we're all *crooks*. How could you believe what any of us told you?"

There was a daily routine: up before dawn; made to rush down the outside corridor by the deputies so we could go to breakfast, then back to the tier for Sick Call for those who needed it and Visitors for those who had them; lunch, waiting, dinner, nothing, lights out. There were a few old issues of *Reader's Digest* floating around, but not much else. Most of the time was spent just waiting: for jail sentences to end, to be taken to court, or to be taken in chains on busses that would take us to prison.

My first breakfast was cereal, powdered milk, powdered eggs, two pieces of toast with margarine and a spoonful of jelly, some fried potatoes and a cup of very weak coffee. We were made to sit at long rows of tables and eat in five minutes, no speaking allowed, as large deputies walked about, watching us.

Across from me, on the other side of our table, there was a Pretty Boy and, across from him, down from me by a few seats, an older career criminal. The kid was new; his nervousness betrayed this, and he was trying to eat, but he kept looking fearfully over at the older man.

I glanced to my right and saw the man openly leering at him.

The boy could take it no longer and suddenly burst out, "Stop looking at me!"

Instantly, the older criminal grabbed his fork and lunged across the table and slashed the kid's face. A river of blood began erupting from the boy's cheek as the kid belatedly raised his hands to protect himself while the older man was quickly seized from behind by two massive deputies.

"Keep eating!" one of them shouted, as they dragged the older man away. Another deputy gently led the kid out to the dispensary as the boy held bloody paper napkins to his face. He'd have his first jail house scar soon and probably wouldn't be so pretty anymore.

Back on our tier, we were allowed out of our cells to mill around and I saw a very big man seated right in the middle of the concrete floor up ahead, where everyone walked around him, very carefully. When I asked my cellmate who that was he told me, "That's a 'Man with Nothing Left to Lose.' You stay away from him."

"Whadaya mean?" I asked.

He lit a cigarette, took a drag off it and passed it to me. It tasted great.

"It means," he said, "that he's got a sentence so long that he's never coming back. He's got, like, three life sentences, one after the other. Normally, they let a man with a life sentence out in twenty years, and that's why they gave him three. If he finishes the first, he does the second and if he finishes that, he does the third. He's in for the whole day. Fuck with him and he'll kill you, 'cause he's got nothing left to lose. What are they going to do? Give him more time? He's already facing all the time there is! You avoid people like that or you won't survive."

I wondered how many thousands of such men our newer laws were creating. With all their longer sentences for sex offenders who haven't been caught yet, were child molesters going to be driven into becoming child killers? *A sentence for murder in some states can now draw less time than one for molesting a child* and, if there is no victim left alive, there's no witness!

A sentencing structure based on anger only endangers the public. We need a return to balanced penalties, penalties that seek to punish as appropriate, but no more. We need to have punishments that also give a man a way to *redeem* himself so that he doesn't think that he has to kill in order to have another chance.

Passover in County Jail

On my second day there my mother came to visit. I was taken to a narrow booth with a stool near a waist-high counter on top of which sat a telephone connecting me to one just like it on her side of the bullet-proof glass window that separated us.

My mother spoke first. "Bob, you're looking well. How are you feeling?"

I didn't want to answer that question truthfully.

She told me that she'd already called officials here, and was going to put forty dollars on my books so I could buy cigarettes and anything else I needed at the jail commissary, but I knew that was just her way of not telling me how very hurt she felt. In the almost twelve months that had elapsed, from the time I gave myself up until now, in spite of numerous times that she and I had gotten together, she had never been able to ask me about my offense and I had never been able to bring myself to speak of it to her.

Other men, with similar offenses, would tell me the same thing, coming from families where denial at the dinner table is the norm because the reality of everyone's lives in their family was too frightening to face. None of them were getting the life they really wanted. And everyone was afraid to admit this, so they substituted pretense for fulfillment and came away with inner bank accounts that were always overdrawn.

Conviction of a sex offense isn't just the failure of the individual who commits it. It's also the failure of his entire family and of everyone who had a role in forming him. As Rupert Ross, a Crown Prosecutor serving North American Indian villages in Canada, has reported in his own books, among traditional peoples a sex offense is also the failure of the entire tribe and must be addressed that way to be healed. They not only ask that the offender undergo a ritual of penance, but that everyone else join him in doing so in order that the entire tribe may be restored to its wholeness.

Offenders aren't banished to faraway prisons there. Native peoples say that's too *light* a penalty. They prefer to keep him within the tribe, so he has to face his shame each day while performing community service and making restitution to the victim and her family by hunting game for them. This doesn't stop until he has earned back his place of honor in the tribe. But, being a culture that dwells in denial, we banish people rather than deal directly with the problems they cause and, as a result, we fail to solve them. And so they continue to occur as our society breaks down, leaving more offenders—and victims—behind.

We need to make some changes. An opportunity for healing has to be a part of the sentence or it is the community that is sentenced to dealing with the offender when he gets back out.

And I needed to change myself. After my visit was over I went back to my tier and grabbed an old copy of some magazine lying on a table, hoping I'd find something in it that would let me escape from facing where I was.

It didn't work. I took it to my cell and, as I lay back on my bunk and tried to read, I couldn't help but be distracted by all the men walking by. In the mirror of their faces I got a nasty look at my own: dirty, cheap men who had squandered their lives by chasing nothing but genital urges in their race toward a bottom that has no bottom. *Depravity.*

Here we all were, ejected from society and sent into this sewer to live. I suddenly understood that this was where The Street ended, that this was where it had always been heading.

I felt sickened with self-loathing and quickly made a silent vow to myself that, somehow, I would find the means to make myself into a person who would *never* have to come back here. That was the moment when I first decided to change.

Later that morning, when my cellmate went to Sick Call and I lay back on the lower bunk with the gate to our cell open, I was just about to doze off when a man appeared there. I blinked my eyes open as he said, "Excuse me."

I sat up in alarm as he continued. "I don't mean to bother you, but I've volunteered to be the Jewish Chaplain's clerk on this tier and from your name I assumed you were Jewish."

There was no reason to be fearful.

He continued. "We're going to be celebrating Passover in a few days and I added you to the list of men who will be transported over to the Main Jail for services. I hope you don't mind."

Passover? In County Jail? The Jewish holiday celebrating liberation from slavery? To even think that my people would reach out to me at a time like this—when I was in this, this *sewer*—was more than I could accept. Tears of gratitude flooded my eyes.

My visitor understood my sudden need for privacy and quietly left my cell as I covered my face with my hands and wept into them.

Don't think that *God* can't be present in a place filled with men who have committed sexual offenses. The question isn't whether God can accept being with a sex offender. The question is whether a sex offender can accept being with God.

Later that week I was put back into a Sheriff's van and driven over to the Main Jail with several others. There were at least fifty inmates present when I arrived and I joined them in sitting at long tables in a large room where small prayer books awaited at each of our places. Up at the front of the room there was a raised platform on top of which, at a long table of their own, sat the Jewish Chaplain, along with several officials and ladies of the Sisterhood that had donated the sacred foods we were about to eat: matzos, gefilte fish, horseradish, bitter herbs, greens, mixed fruit and nuts, a lamb's shank and roast chicken.

When the Rabbi began the service, I was shocked to see that virtually all of the other men around me—murderers, rapists, thieves, embezzlers— knew how to read the passages written in Hebrew. Only I, with my law school education and master's degree, did not know the language of my own people.

A wish suddenly welled up within me: If only I could have the time to really learn my religion!

Some wishes are heard as prayers. And those are granted.

*   *   *

Why Repeat Offenders Keep Repeating

At 4:00 A.M. a couple of weeks later, I was shackled in chains to a long line of other prisoners and loaded onto a sheriff's bus and driven out to the intake facility for the state's prison system. There, one of its many penal institutions would be picked for me after counselors had gone over my court file. There are all kinds of prisons for all kinds of men. Some house factories, inside of which men work. Others have educational programs or major medical services. Some are just human warehouses, and the first task of the prison system is to determine which kind of institution would be most appropriate for each person sentenced into its custody.

Immediately upon entering the facility, our chains were removed as guards looked on and directed us to a long counter where one of the clerks turned out to be a former client of mine: a tall mildly-overweight man in his fifties with salt and peppered hair. I'd worked on his sentencing hearing and lost in my bid to keep him out of prison. Now, he was serving time and, as his prison work-assignment, hand-stenciling prisoners' names onto the tabs of what would become their file folders. "See how good my workmanship is?" he asked, hopefully.

He had formerly been the vice president of a statewide bank.

Various other clerks filled out papers on us as we were asked to state our name, date of birth and next of kin. I was then taken in a long line with the other men down a long corridor at the end of which there were three landings of jail cells, each cell housing two men. The cell I was given was on the third landing and already had its other resident: a tall, lanky man in his forties with thinning black hair who hailed from some rural town and was back in prison again. A repeat offender—he said he was a car thief— he was happy to be coming back and talked about the lieutenant he had worked for in prison as if the man had been his father.

He schooled me not to walk next to the edge of our tier when I went to chow with all of the other men.

"Why not?" I asked, naively.

He snorted to himself as we were released for the next meal and clawed our way through everyone to take the stairs down. "So you don't get pushed off by someone who wants to be a 'bad killer' now that he's in here."

I accepted his advice.

After the meal, when we were back in our cell, he lay back on a pillow on the lower bunk and I stood, leaning against the wall across from him and asked him what would happen to me inside this place.

"You'll wait," he replied, "like all the rest of us."

"For what?"

"Until you've been seen by a counselor and assigned to a prison." He reached into his shirt pocket and pulled out a small sack of cigarette tobacco, then some papers and sat up to roll himself one. He looked over at me. "Want it?"

I shook my head 'no' and pulled out a pack I'd bought at County Jail.

His eyes bulged wide. "Store-bought?"

I smiled and offered him one, which he gladly accepted, and we both lit up as he told me things the public never hears about why a person is sent to one kind of prison rather than another: how likely he is to escape!

At the top of the heap were places from which it was virtually impossible to break out: behind gun towers manned by officers with loaded rifles, on walls so high that you couldn't jump over them, standing on soil so impregnated with motion detectors that you couldn't crawl out without being heard. They were called Level Four institutions.

Level Three was a place where the soil didn't have those devices, but still had walls and gun towers with armed guards.

Level Two had a tall chain link fence around it—and, of course, gun towers.

Level One might be a fire fighting camp, up in the forest, with no fence at all. "Just a line you never cross," my cellmate said. And when he saw the look of hunger cross my face, he laughed to himself and added: "Everyone with a long sentence to do starts at Level Four."

The look vanished.

"Listen," he said. "These people aren't stupid! They know that if you had a chance right now, you'd run. So what they do with a new man is put him somewhere at the start of his sentence where he can't possibly escape."

He paused to take another drag from his smoke.

"Later," he went on, reaching over to tap his cigarette on the edge of the sink, "after you've been down a while, they'll move ya. To a less-secure institution, and let you get used to that. And then they'll move you again—in your case, probably a couple of years before you're ready to go home. In that last place, frankly, you could probably just walk away if you wanted to, it's that casual."

I thought about that for a moment. "Does anyone ever do so?"

He laughed to himself and said, "Nah!"

"Why not?"

"Hell!" he replied, tapping his cigarette again. And then, in an aside, he said, "Better than letting the ashes fall on the floor. It's our house now." I stopped flicking mine on the floor and he went on. "The penalty for escape is two years and ya only got two left to do! You've already been down; the worst is behind you; you know you can do the time because you've already done more than two, and you just don't."

He added that there were always a couple of exceptions: "Fools, or guys who just want to get caught and be given more time."

I looked at him, puzzled. "Given more time? Why would anyone want that?"

"Well," he said, looking away from me for a moment, "maybe they ain't got nothin' on the outside."

I couldn't accept that. "But still," I began to say, then he cut me off angrily.

"Look—it's 'three hots and a cot'. Ya get fed three times a day. Ya get a bed to sleep in that's not wet in the wintertime and not crawling with bugs in the summer. Ya get medical care and dental care when you need it. Hell, these eyeglasses I got," and he reached over to pick up a pair resting next to him, "*they* made them for me."

I foolishly asked him how many times he'd been in and he looked away, as if staring into his memories.

"Three."

How to Get Help in Prison

I wouldn't see a counselor right away. In the world of prisons no one is in a rush to do anything because, if there's anything an inmate has lots of, it's time and jobs that normally would be done outside in a day took a week to get done here. So I began to wait. The cell was so small and, because there wasn't much room in it to do anything else, I spent most of my time there up on my bunk.

And slept. I began to sleep a lot during the day, so much that I began to wonder if maybe I could sleep away my whole ten-year sentence. *Maybe I'd just wake up and find the whole thing had only been a dream.*

Other than going to chow three times a day, there was nothing else to do. It got so boring I sometimes went to chow even when I wasn't hungry, and ate anyhow, just for something to do. Einstein was right: time is relative. You can sit down at your computer and knock off some e-mail and be astounded when you find that *two full hours* have just sped by. But when your computer takes sixty seconds to boot-up, it feels like sixty *minutes*!

Prison is like boot-up time. People say: "He only did five years." *You* try waiting for your life to boot-up again for five years!

I finally got to see my intake counselor: a man in his late forties with dark hair and a heavily-lined face, who occupied a small cubicle barely big enough for his desk, a small office chair, and a folding metal chair on my side. He sat behind the desk in his shirtsleeves and a tie and my file was in front of him: the one that had my name hand-stenciled onto its tab now.

"Sit down," he said, when I came to his doorway.

I did as he said.

He peered down at the file a moment, then looked up and began asking me questions meant to assess what kind of person I was likely to become now, for it would be his job to determine the kind of prison to which I'd be sent. Part of that job was keeping the guards there safe, by not sending them the kind of person with which they usually don't deal, who belongs somewhere else, with other kinds of guards.

He wanted to see if I accepted any responsibility for my crime or if, like many others, I just tried to blame some one else, like my ex-wife or, worse yet, the child. I've seen cases like that: where a nine-year old girl has been sexually abused by her stepfather and he claims it happened because 'she came in while I was in the bathroom,' or similar lame excuses. They're poison in a place like this. Come into prison and tell your intake counselor that it's not your fault and he'll just throw you back into the hopper, to be processed like dog meat.

The same is true if you come in complaining about the system: "I had a lousy lawyer." Even if it's true, you'd do best to save it for the time when you can file an appeal, not use it as your excuse for being here. Counselors see too many who claim innocence when the record screams out their guilt, and they have a very short fuse for it as they are part of the same team that investigated you and they believe in that team.

If you know anyone who gets convicted of a sex offense—or if you know one of their relatives—and you want them to get help while they're in prison, this is what you tell them: be respectful when you're called in by your first counselor, answering in full and without any excuses every question that you're asked, and express some sense of remorse for what you did that led to your being sent here for having hurt someone else!

What the counselor is looking at is your *attitude*. Show a good one, be sincere and truthful, and he can set you on the road to places with resources that will be made available to you as you do your time. Show a bad one, come in whining and complaining—or trying to charm or impress him—and, well, you read about what happens to sex offenders in prisons where they probably shouldn't have been sent. 'Mistakes happen,' as they say.

It's up to each prisoner whether they happen to him.

"Never tell anyone what your crime is," my counselor concluded, "or you might get killed for it! Your offense is at the bottom of the criminal hierarchy. When other men ask you what you're in for, say 'embezzlement,' or something like that. Otherwise you won't make it. Many of these men have been sexually molested as kids themselves, or have sisters who were, or kids themselves that they worry about now. They'll take it out on you if they find out why you're here."

He was saving my life, but I couldn't see it at the time. All I could think was that, if imprisonment is this dangerous, why do they put us here instead of in a mental hospital? What we do isn't a capital offense. Is it just in the *hope* that we'll be killed? The result is that many men like us never even try to get help for their offense, so no one finds out about it. As a consequence, when our sentences are over, we return to your community, just as we were when we left it. And people blame *us* for re-offending?

We need special yards in prisons, for people like us, so we can openly seek treatment, and in some places they're beginning to have them. We need them throughout the nation's prison system.

My counselor stared intensely at me as he ended our interview. "Remember what I said. I'm warning you. Don't talk about your crime."

I nodded in agreement, got up and left his tiny cubicle to go back to my cell and wait until it was time for me to go to the prison he'd chosen for me.

The Power of My Life

I lost my cell mate the next day: they shipped him back to the same institution he'd been in before.

He was so *happy* when he got the news!

It was back to waiting until my turn to leave came, back to lying on my bunk all day between meals, with nothing to do and no one to talk to now: with nothing but the shredded trappings of a 'self,' and even they soon peeled away. As I lay there and looked at the ceiling I soon began to see pictures of my life going by like a merry-go-round, from childhood to now, one after another.

They didn't stop. When the cycle reached where I was now, it started all over again. Just when I thought that I'd really go nuts, all of a sudden I saw something in myself behind those images—that they all came from what I can only call an 'inner projector' that causes them to appear.

My whole life was just a projection—*from something else within me!*

I quickly named that something the Power of My Life and knew it would not abandon me; that this was not to be the way my life ended.

Another vision began to appear on the ceiling—of a street corner at the bottom of a large hill in Hollywood, atop which sat the Vedanta Temple to which I'd so often gone while struggling to understand myself during those dark years when that 'Other' within me was carrying me all over the city all night long.

Now, I suddenly realized, this was where my life was going to go. I was going to come back to that spot! Some time, some way, I was going to return there. It was a statement from the Power of My Life that I was going to survive prison. It was a *Promise!*

But would I have any more answers by then?

More days of empty waiting followed. In desperation for something to do—for something to read, just to get my mind off things—I broke line after coming back from chow one time and bolted through the open doors of the Interfaith Chapel.

Glancing around quickly, I saw what I was looking for, over to one side. On top of a plain wooden table in the corner, there was a whole stack of paperback copies of The Bible.

I snatched one and took it back to my cell. And I began to read it from the very first page.

"*In the beginning...*"

I read the stories of The Creation, The Flood, of Adam and Eve, Cain and Abel, Noah, Abraham, Isaac and Jacob.

Then I came to *The Story of Joseph*. He, too, had been imprisoned for a sex offense: attempted rape. They'd locked him away for thirteen years.

The charge was false, we're told that, but so what? Thirteen years is a big piece of time, especially when one is young, as Joseph was. He'd only been a kid when he went in—seventeen—the youngest child of jealous older brothers who'd sold him into slavery where he found work in the house of a wealthy man. But the man's wife coveted Joseph and he would not lie with her, for he was loyal to his master. That made the woman spiteful and in her anger she lied and said that Joseph had taken her by force. And down he went into the House of Prison, into his own underworld.

But God smiled upon him there and gave him the gift of interpreting dreams, and he soon gained a reputation for doing so among Pharaoh's officials. When the great Pharaoh had dreams that no one else could interpret, it was Joseph for whom they finally sent.

And Joseph interpreted the dreams of Pharaoh, and warned him that, after seven years of plenty that were coming to all of Egypt, there would be seven cruel ones when the land would be gripped by famine, advising Pharaoh to prepare for them by setting aside excess food during the good times. Pharaoh listened to Joseph and appointed him to that task, placing him at his right hand over all others.

The Great Famine came as Joseph predicted, and from all over the region people flocked to Egypt for food, willing to pay any price. Joseph set the price and made Pharaoh even wealthier, and Pharaoh smiled upon Joseph.

One day it was Joseph's older brothers who stood before him to ask for food and they didn't recognize him, for instead of a beardless youth they now faced a fully-bearded man in his thirties, a man of great power and influence second only to that of the Great Pharaoh.

But Joseph recognized them and when he could no longer stand his concealment he broke into tears and revealed himself. They froze in terror. This man could have them *killed* merely by nodding to his guards!

Joseph saw their fear and comforted them. "*I am no longer angry for what you did to me when I was a child, for I now know that it was not you— but God, acting through you—who sent me here.*"

Could the answer to what really causes any tragedy, from avalanches to murders, really be that far away? I've met people who have said so, and seen it comfort them to get past enormous tragedies that have come into their lives. And I've met others who insist that such an idea is mere foolishness, and remain drowning in their own bitterness.

I chose to stand with the first group. Looking inside myself, I saw all the hatred that I was still carrying toward my ex-wife over her having left me for someone else, all the anger that was still mine over her having testified as a witness for the prosecution in sending me to prison. And I could not accept the idea that I had wrecked my whole life this completely—and my daughter's—all by myself. I'd never chosen to become a child molester. I had never chosen to be ruled by such an urge. I'd never knowingly sought to harm my own daughter, although I knew that I had harmed her.

Again and again, I saw it in my life: that this was something that was done to me, it was not something that I designed. I was imprisoned long before I came to this place. And I couldn't live with the idea that I had made all this happen by myself.

I put down *The Bible*, got off my bunk and walked over to my cell door. Gripping its bars with all my strength, I prayed for the first time since I was a child.

"Please! Let me also come to know that it was You who sent me here, so I may also come back without hatred for anyone."

Not even for myself.

*   *   *

How to Protect Your Children

1. Tell your members of Congress and the state legislature that you want convicted sex offenders to be given sentences that include treatment before they get out.

2. Tell your members of Congress and the state legislature that you want sentences that leave a man with a chance to come back when he earns it.

3. If you know anyone sent to prison as a sex offender, tell them to to accept responsibility for being there when they see their first counselor so they can get all the help they will need.

*   *   *

Questions to Consider

1. Should every criminal sentence include a chance for the person to redeem themselves?

2. Are sex offenses solely the failure of the person committing them, or are they also the failure of the entire tribe? Is our culture too morally passive and, therefore, also to blame in some way?

3. Is the source of tragedy to be found just in the world and within ourselves? Or are there larger forces that also act? What would you tell a person, to comfort them in the face of enormous personal loss?

4. What would you tell yourself in the same kind of situation? Where would you find your own refuge?

Chapter Five

Evil or Ill?

From Cure to Control

Treatment for sex offenders is not a new art. In the early part of the twentieth century, neurosurgeons simply cut out that part of the person's brain that had to do with the sex drive. According to Canadian sex therapist W.L. Marshall, one of the pioneers of newer treatments, a group of German surgeons were the leading advocates of that earlier method. When they later found that the number of patients who committed new sex crimes following surgery was still no lower than that of those who had been spared the surgeon's knife, the human brain as the sole location of our sex drive was dropped, along with that form of therapy.

Surgical castration was popular for a while in Europe, and at first looked like it promised success as many patients went back to the community and remained arrest-free. But then someone noticed that the patients included a number of homosexuals, who hadn't raped women or molested children in the first place, which presumably accounted for why they weren't "repeating" those crimes now. When they were removed from the follow-up statistics, early optimism quickly faded as the readjusted figures showed that almost half of all the remaining sex offenders who had been castrated still continued to masturbate or have intercourse, something anyone who knew history could have told them:

It had been known from Greek times, and probably before, that castration did not eliminate sexual desire and that a castrate who had preserved his penis was, under certain circumstances, capable of having erections…and could even be aroused to a kind of ejaculation…

p.249, *SEX IN HISTORY* by Reay Tannahill (1992)

It should not have been surprising, then, that while a 1968 study indicated that Danish castrates did stop committing any more sex crimes, a third of their number continued to commit other crimes, which suggested that their underlying aggression hadn't been changed. And when hormones became commercially available, permitting a patient to cancel the effect of castration, there seemed no point to continue using this method and it was discarded.

Psychologists didn't do much better when they applied conventional therapy. One California program for sex offenders had a 19 percent failure rate among its patients over a three-year follow-up period. When it was extended to five years, the re-offense rate jumped to 26 percent and the program became politically unsupportable.

The problem, it was later learned, was that therapists were seeking the wrong goal: trying to *cure* a problem that would be more successfully addressed if it was just placed under control. As one leading official in the state mental health department put it:

> …there appears to be an emerging consensus among treatment providers…that the overall goal of treatment is one of management or control, not cure. This rejects the notion that sex offending is an *illness* from which one will recover and that successful treatment will result in the elimination of the disorder. Instead, it suggests that successful interventions are those that train offenders to reduce exposure to situations that place them at risk for reoffense…"

Marques, et. al, "The Sex Offender Treatment and Evaluation Project, Fourth Report to the Legislature in Response to PC 1365," Division of State Hospitals, Department of Mental Health, October, 1991, p. 5.

A lot of things can't be "cured." No cures exist for AIDS, diabetes, schizophrenia and numerous other medical and psychiatric conditions. But they can be controlled so that the individual afflicted with them can continue to live in the community without endangering himself or anyone else. In spite of the sometimes sensationalistic reporting given to the most extreme (and, fortunately, rare) cases, recent statistics show that many sex offenders can be taught how to manage their own behavior. The author, for example, is in his fifteenth year of remaining free from re-offending at the time of this writing.

When a new pilot program designed to pursue *self-control* instead of cure was carefully tried out by the State of California, the re-offense rate for its graduates was reduced by two-thirds. Sex offending might not be curable, but it could be controlled—for the rest of the former offender's life—by the offender.

Barriers to Treatment

Treatment doesn't begin until we're ready to really face ourselves. And if you are a sex offender in a time when the climate all around the subject has been shaped primarily by the victims of sexual offenses, facing yourself may be very hard to do. Victims, quite naturally, choose to utterly demonize sex offenders and they have enormous political influence.

The result, as this chapter will show, is that many of our treatment programs have been hobbled by laws that don't mean to heal anybody, but only seek vengeance.

Obviously if, as their sponsors believe, punishment really is the answer, there wouldn't be a sex offender anywhere in the world today. Over the last twenty years, punishment has so reshaped criminal law that penalties have been raised to the skies, yet sex offenders continue to exist and their crimes continue to be as awful as before. The fact that sex offenders are fewer in number only means that punishment has done as much as it can but it has not eliminated the problem.

Punishment alone, therefore, is not the answer. But it is part of the answer. I know of no better place to put a convicted sex offender than in prison for, like a monastic cell, it leaves him alone with his problems so that he finally has no choice but to face them.

A Certain Kind of Walk

Not long after I saw my counselor at that prison intake facility, I was shackled in chains and put on a prison bus that took me to a penitentiary so new that it was still being built when I arrived. It was one of those newer joints: pre-fabricated, with reinforced concrete walls. The walls were bolted together to make buildings inside of which there were two stories of cells on three sides. On the fourth there was a two-story guards' office with a glass-enclosed control booth. The guards spoke to us from inside the control booth through loudspeakers.

The walls around the prison weren't up yet, so it sat under the protection of a ring of gun towers and razor-wire fences that could cut a man in two if he tried to climb over them. There wasn't a tree or even a bush anywhere in sight—either in our yard or beyond those fences—so there was nothing that could hide a man from gunfire if he somehow made it out. They'd removed all of the vegetation before they built the place, leaving the earth as barren as our lives now.

And yet, there was something so subversively *appealing* about it all. Like death, prison accepts everyone. No one is too bad to be turned away. Or too good. And, once you're in prison, you don't have to care anymore. No one expects anything of you again. You can give up, if you want to, and a lot of men do.

I wasn't supposed to have been sent here. My intake counselor had rec-ommended a better place for me, but out of clumsily making a sexual advance on a younger inmate on my tier at the intake facility, other men quickly deduced that I was a child molester. Almost immediately, I found myself facing so much hostility that I had to ask staff for protection and they just put me on the next bus out of there. Now I was at a place that looked like the end of the world.

So that's another lesson that anyone going to prison should learn: *don't become a problem for staff or they'll send you to a place full of nothing but problems.*

I was taken to my new cell by a guard, the door was electronically slid open and I entered carrying the blankets, sheets and a pillow I'd been given. Then the door closed behind me.

My cellmate was lying back against a pillow on the lower bunk: a grizzled, older man from a rural background doing a life sentence who'd been in before. He gave me his name and asked for mine.

But I felt too ashamed of who I'd been to even want to be him anymore, so I quickly searched within myself for some other. The memory of my grandfather on my father's side came forth—a gentle man who had been the only one in my family who'd ever seemed as if he'd really loved me just for being me. And I decided to become him.

"*Jake*," I said. And I've done my best to honor that name ever since. Soon, I'd do what many of the other convicts did, and grow a long beard to hide behind, to keep anyone from seeing my face.

To keep me from having to face myself.

My new cellmate got up off his bed and shook my hand heartily. "How much time they give ya, Jake?"

"Ten years," I said.

"A dime!" he exclaimed. "That ain't nothin'. Been down over ten already."

Later, he would point out men who had been in prison two and three times that amount. Now, he opened his shirt pocket and pulled out a pack of cigarettes to offer me one, then lit one for himself. "Whatcha in for?"

"Embezzlement," I replied flatly.

My cellmate said that I'd be given work soon, in the kitchen at first and then in a prison factory later. Those were the only kinds of jobs they had there, and it seemed awfully bleak.

It wasn't long until his prediction came true and I was assigned to the chow hall, working from early in the morning until early in the afternoon. The rest of the day was my own and I used it to walk the large oval track around our yard in a futile attempt to get rid of the heavy clouds of depression that had now begun to hang over me.

I bowed my head under them as I walked and kept my hands plunged deeply into my pockets. For my life had come to nothing and an ever-hungry regret ate away at me over how I imagined my daughter might wind up, now that I wasn't there to take care of her. Had I not failed as her father it would not have come to this and I knew it, and that made my pain even worse.

A moment kept coming back to me after my wife had confronted me and taken the child home with her. It was two days later, when she and her new boyfriend came over to my place to get all of my daughter's belongings now that she'd be living only with them. They came to get her clothes, her toys, anything else she had, all of which had been kept in the small bedroom that had been hers in my apartment.

Knowing they were coming, I'd gathered all her things together that morning so I wouldn't have to think about what it would be like when I'd have to face the two of them later that day.

Just as arranged, they showed up, and then told me they didn't need my help in taking anything down to their car. It didn't take long until they were finished.

Afterwards, I went back into my daughter's bedroom and looked around. It was totally empty. Nothing was there except a feeling of sadness. That's when it hit me. That's when I realized that I had lost her forever. It was in that moment that I sat down in the middle of the floor and then threw myself face down onto the pile carpet, to bury my face in the places where she had walked and I just cried, and cried and cried.

It was the same pain that continued to hang over me now and I quickly learned that I couldn't escape it, either through walking the prison yard, retreating into my dreams at night or even in watching TV.

At four o'clock every day, we all had to get back into our cells to be counted, so the prison could be sure that no one had escaped. Men who had them were allowed to watch their small television sets, and my cellmate always turned on his. There was nothing but talk shows everyday, and every talk show that year seemed to focus on nothing but sexual misconduct, especially within the family.

Having to listen to it was like hearing two angry cats clawing at each other inside of me. I wanted to scream at my cellmate to turn it off, but I couldn't say a thing as my counselor's advice continually replayed itself in my mind: "Never tell anyone what your crime is or you might get killed for it."

My pain followed me into the night, where I dreamed troublesome dreams that often woke me up.

I walked the Yard every day in mourning for my life and it wasn't long before some of the men began taking bets on how soon I'd hang myself. For they had seen other men take that same kind of walk and they knew where it led.

It surely would have but for one thing. After I'd been there just over four months, my sentence would automatically come up for reconsideration by the court and I knew it. That was what kept me alive. They shipped me back to County Jail for the hearing and I hoped with all my heart that the court might change my sentence to one of probation, allowing me to go free under supervision in the community. But a few days before my case was to be heard, I was told that wasn't likely to happen. A former professional associate of mine had spoken to the judge on my behalf and now came to see me.

"He wants you to do hard time," she told me, assessing what he had said to her in chambers. My nerves cracked under the pressure, and that night I began to hear voices urging me to kill myself. I fought with them until I realized that, before the night was over, they were going to win.

"Deputy!" I called out fearfully.

One responded right away and I broke down completely as I described what was going on within me.

Staff immediately moved me into the County Jail's mental health ward, where I was given medication. As soon as I was stabilized enough, I was taken to court and my case was heard.

The hearing was as brief as it was unrewarding. The Judge said he had reviewed the report he had requested from prison officials as to how I was doing and they had rated me as *adjusting satisfactorily.*

"I see no reason to disturb the sentence."

I was sent back to my penitentiary but, because of that near-suicidal episode, transferred to a nearby prison medical facility where I finally began to get help. I was ready for it now and I welcomed it.

Can Sex Offenders Help Sex Offenders?

Ever since I had been assaulted by that convicted sex offender when I was thirteen—and then 'trained' over the next year by an older boy at school—I had been driven to chase teenage boys. Now, for reasons I couldn't even remotely understand, I had also been driven to harm my daughter. What might I be made to do next? And by who? By what? What 'crazy' drive was within me that could take over my life and force it to go in the direction it wanted? How could I possibly hope to have a life unless I got whatever it was under control?

I put in a request to see a psychotherapist and it was granted. I was sent to see a psychologist who told me she had formerly treated the child victims of sexual abuse and now sought to treat men like me so that none of us would ever harm another child again. Once a week, she permitted many of us under her care to meet among ourselves in a nearby conference room where we were allowed to run our own therapy group.

"I can't get you into it," she told me. "That's up to the men. But I can nominate you for their consideration and you'll be summoned to appear before them. If you can convince them that you belong in their group, they'll admit you as a member. It's up to you."

She said that what they'd insist upon most was total honesty on my part. There'd be no admittance if I tried to deny my crimes, or place responsibility for them on anyone but myself.

I asked her to put my name forth and a week later I was called to their meeting. Upon entering, I found a dozen men seated on both sides of a long conference table: rapists, child molesters, sex offenders of every kind, maybe even child killers. Instantly I knew that if I tried to lie about anything it wouldn't work—for these men had probably told the same lies and would see right through me.

A man that I'll call William was their chairman: a fiftyish man with a gray Van Dyke beard who sat in a perfectly starched-and-ironed sky-blue prison shirt and brand-new dark blue jeans at the far end of table. With clothes like that, he obviously had juice in this prison and knew how to get things done. I could see why he was the chairman.

He was smoking a pipe as I came in and took it out as he smiled and said: "Welcome to our group."

I stood at my end of the table. "Thank you."

"Why don't you tell us what you were convicted for?"

"I molested my daughter, several times."

One of the men asked, "Do you take responsibility for what you did?"

"I do."

Then the questions began to come at me from all of the others, hard and fast.

"Why did you do it?

"Did you ever consider the damage you were causing her?"

"Why didn't you seek professional help?"

And, finally, the most difficult question of all: "Why didn't you stop?"

Snapshot memories flickered past in my mind, leaving painful after-trails.

"Why didn't you stop? Tell us!"

All of my accumulated pain was about to come down.

"A part of me was too angry to stop," I tried to explain.

But the men weren't buying it and tears began to stream down my face as I quickly amended my answer.

"I was too weak to protect her—from myself."

The pain fell on me like an avalanche. Instantly, I covered my face with my hands as I sobbed into them. "And I'm so very *ashamed* of myself!"

Somebody handed me a open box of facial tissues that was nearby and moments later I was quietly asked to wait outside while the members balloted among themselves. I thought I'd seen tears in the eyes of a couple of the other men as I left, but I couldn't be sure. When the door was opened again, I walked back in and returned to my end of the table to wait as William recited the group's decision.

"We decline to accept you."

It was like a blow to the pit of my stomach, but I held it in and politely responded, "That is your right and I accept it. Thank you for considering me."

I turned to leave and grasped the doorknob.

"Wait!"

It was William's voice. When I turned around to face him, all of the men were smiling at me now.

"That was the last test," he said, gently. "We give it to all the men, to make sure they'll accept our authority. We welcome you as our newest member."

I was in!

With their help, I soon learned that sexual misconduct is the final product of a chain of mental events. The first link in that chain is an *impulse* that ripens into an *idea* and finally becomes an *action*. Impulses are harmless, everyone has them: a man sees a pretty girl and, instantly, has a sexual impulse toward her. But, since it's only an impulse, his reasoning mind steps in and restrains him from doing anything about it, so the impulse evaporates and he goes on with his life as if the impulse had never occurred.

In a sex offender that doesn't happen. Instead, the impulse becomes an *idea* so alluring that he falls under its spell and he makes a *plan* to act on it, and then the *act* results. He becomes drawn to act by the hypnotic nature of the idea his own mind has formed. That's where he becomes intoxicated; that's when the reasoning part of his mind begins to shut down.

As I learned from these men, the earlier we choose to halt this process, the easier it is to do so. *Impulses* can be escaped. A man can make himself start thinking of something else. If he doesn't, and allows it to become an *idea*, he's in danger, and so is his potential victim, because now the impulse is gathering strength and soon will be harder to stop as a plan starts being formed.

We called this process our Chain of Causes, with each link leading to the next. Breaking that chain—the sooner, the better—became our motto. We meant to take back control of our minds by assuming responsibility for what we allowed them to do.

Some people believe that if you let a bunch of 'sex offenders' meet together, all they'll do is 'compare notes' and come up with better ways to get victims. I even know of some politicians who preach this fear.

Active sex offenders might: people who are still looking for victims all the time probably would ask each other how to do it better. But former sex offenders now in recovery would not. They've already decided to take control back over their life. If they compare notes on anything, it's on how to stay in control.

I've now visited almost a dozen groups since that time on the outside. Never have I heard anyone suggest that the time be used to go back to what we've been. Responsible groups all have the same rules: no 'sex' talk. No attempt to get anyone excited. Clinical terms alone are all that is permitted when discussing a crime we have committed. Anyone who refused to obey those rules would have their membership terminated. There are no exceptions.

Thanks to my therapist, I soon gave up the hope that I had been cherishing of reuniting with my daughter after I was released from prison. I had mentioned it at one of my sessions with the doctor and she helped me see that it was only a nice daydream I was having.

"Look," she said, gently. "When you get out, your daughter is going to be in adolescence. Do you really think that a young girl at that sensitive stage of her life is really going to want a father around who has just gotten out of prison for doing what you did?"

Even I could see what she meant.

My therapist suggested, instead, that it might be much better if I wrote a short note to my daughter right then, letting her know that I still loved her, but saying a final 'good-bye.' Since Christmas was approaching, she suggested I buy a nice card in the prison store, volunteering to mail it for me.

"Keep the note short," she said.

I followed her advice.

Twelve Step Programs

The teachings of Alcoholics Anonymous also helped me. I was given library privileges and, the first day I went there, I found a book published by that organization that spoke right to me. AA uses a method called the

Twelve Step Program that begins with an admission that one's life is out of control, and destructive.

I was able to admit that.

They went on to suggest that we all have some *Higher Power* to which we can turn to help us place our life back under control. That higher power could be God, or one's center of consciousness, or anything else a person finds that he can use to give him extra strength when he needs it. For some who aren't at all religious, the group in Alcoholics Anonymous becomes their higher power.

Having already had that shattering experience with the *I Ching* on sentencing day, I certainly believed that higher powers existed. As a result, what Alcoholics Anonymous was talking about made perfect sense to me. The only problem was that, since I wasn't an alcoholic, I wasn't sure AA's methods would work for me.

That was then. As I would later learn, the same methods used by Alcoholics Anonymous have now been adapted for successful use with addicts of all kinds: from compulsive gamblers to narcotics users. Not much before my discovery of AA's book, several sexual compulsives in the United States had already started using their own adaptation of this program to tame their own urges. Since then, over half a dozen national and worldwide organizations that help anyone struggling with what are usually less serious sexual problems—such as excessive masturbation, compulsive use of pornography or constantly going to prostitutes—use a similar adaptation. (*See:* **Self-Recovery Organizations** in the Readers Resources section of this book.) Many government mental health programs for serious sex offenders also include an approach similar to AA's within their own spectrum of therapies.

This is not to say that all sexual offenders are merely sex addicts who can place their urges under voluntary control. Where a sexual offense includes severe physical violence or is based upon urges too strong to be overcome by AA's Twelve Step Method, deeper therapies have to be used that often require the recipient to be kept within a secure facility over an extended period of time. Or given chemical means to suppress his sexual urges (chemical castration). But, for many of us, the Twelve Step approach helps; as I would soon find out, it would help me, too.

Human After All

Several months later I was transferred to another prison, a protective custody facility for the state's most vulnerable prisoners: people who would be killed or ruthlessly victimized by other prisoners in any other penal institution. Among its inhabitants could be found convicted judges, cops, prosecutors; gang dropouts, inmates so emotionally impaired they would be preyed upon endlessly at a regular prison, sex offenders and, in a separate yard, younger prisoners who looked too pretty for their own safety and would be raped until they committed suicide anywhere else.

It was 'live and let live' here. Nobody made any trouble because they knew that, if they did, they would be transferred to a regular facility. As a result, everybody got along.

Because of my law background, I was immediately invited by one of the more influential prisoners on the yard to become his cellmate in exchange for helping him appeal his sentence. A large Italian man who liked to eat, his cell had shelves built on to the walls that held every kind of food sold by the prison canteen, and he generously shared everything he had. I probably gained five pounds from helping him.

As I worked on his case, we got to know each other. One night, I told him why I had really been sent to prison, but changed the story a bit to make it look as if I'd been framed by my ex-wife. I was still too ashamed to tell anyone but doctors and other men in a therapy group the full truth.

That was a big mistake, for word got around and, two days later, someone approached me on the yard and said that I could have her killed, just because she had snitched on me.

I suddenly realized what I'd almost done. That night, I corrected it by telling my cellmate the rest: that the charges brought against me had been completely deserved, that I had molested my own daughter. It was just after lights out, and he was lying on his side on the upper bunk.

He leaned over and looked down at me. "You poor lost soul," he said, quietly. "You poor, poor lost soul."

That was when I began to suspect how very far into the darkness I had gone.

Was I the worst of such men? I had to know. Because there were so many of us here—where it was safe to talk among ourselves—I went out into the prison yard to meet some of my peers. The first thing I learned is that, as sex offender Psychologist Anna C. Salter writes, there are two kinds of sex offenders:

- The Opportunists, who really aren't sex offenders as much as people with weak morals who merely find themselves in a tempting situation, like the burglar who breaks into an apartment and finds an attractive woman there, so he decides to rape her, and

- The Compulsives, people who act out because of an inner urge they haven't yet learned how to control.

The second thing I learned is why some sex offenders in prison don't choose to reform. They don't think that anything is wrong with them.

There was the Satanist who had been convicted of ritually killing a fourteen-year-old boy. A bulky man in his thirties, with a dark little beard and very dark eyes, he confided that, "Satan made me do it! He promised that, if I'd do it, he'd always be with me!"

Presumably for life without the possibility of parole, since that is what he got.

There was the child molester who stalked little girls until he knew where they lived and when they were home alone. He'd show up there and tell the child that he was from the "health department" and needed to examine her.

He told me he was caught when the father of one of the children came home early.

"He grabbed a butcher knife and tried to kill me!"

Terrified, he ran out of the apartment house, with the outraged father in hot pursuit, angrily wielding the huge knife.

Just as the molester reached the street, a black-and-white police car happened to round the corner and he plunged in its way and stopped it.

"I did it!" he told them. "Take me in!"

They did—for twenty years.

Twice I was later celled with rapists. One had committed his crime while the woman's little daughter was in the same room and looked on in shock. He said that he thought it was funny to see the fear on the little girl's face as he forced himself upon her mother.

The other was even more menacing. When he found that I was reading books on boating, a popular fantasy interest for many inmates, he asked me if you can "rent" a boat.

"Certainly," I said, putting down the book to look at him. He was in his late twenties, with a trim build and light brown hair; someone who would be attractive to many women.

A snarl could be heard in his voice as he exclaimed, "That's what I'm going to do when I get out of here: rent myself a boat, on some lake, and take some *bitch* out on it, *and rape the fuck out of her!*"

I'm sure he meant it.

Then there was the self-educated intellectual who simply insisted that he had a natural right to go after what he called Little Lolitas. Bespectacled and in his fifties, he said, "There have always been sexual relations between some adults and children, everywhere in the world, and there always will be. People don't have to be limited to having sex just with other adults. Sexual pleasure isn't just one note, but a whole chorus of them."

It was his argument that the only thing that made sex a crime was the country in which it took place, and there is some truth to that. According to one study, rape is only rape when a man does it in some countries and the victim is a woman. In other countries, if the victim is a boy, that's not so. Similarly, unless the child is under age sixteen in some European, Asian and African countries, age fifteen in others, fourteen in yet others and thirteen in Spain or twelve in the Philippines, the crime of child molestation hasn't been committed.

And not all countries punish sex offenses with equal severity. In one European country, a sin of the flesh can draw a fine of just under five U.S. dollars while, in a neighboring state, the same offense is worth fines in the thousands of dollars.

Anxious to win me to his side, he urged me to read the man he considered his champion, French intellectual Michel Foucault, one of that country's most celebrated thinkers. "He explains why we have the sexual rules we live by today."

I did so. I got a hold of Foucault's *The History of Sexuality, Volume I,* which argues that sex didn't become a police matter until the Sovereign realized that population is the source of wealth; the more people, the more workers. As a result of this realization, any sexual practice that didn't result in reproduction was suddenly called a *perversion.*

From my friend's viewpoint, the only basis for morality is economics—when, in fact, morals are really another name for our values. They are absolutely fundamental to who we are as a people because they are what makes us a people: in a storm-tossed world, they're our wind-shelter against chaos. The person who doesn't have them winds up here, in prison.

However, out of my talks with this man, what I finally realized was that there have always been men (and women) like us and, presumably, there always will be. We are a recurrent sexual direction that has appeared in virtually every group of people that has ever existed. What that suggests is that there always will be people like us in every generation. We are not just today's departure from the norm. We have always been and always will be something beyond the norm. We are part of what it means to say there is a *human* species, hard as that may be to accept. Human sexuality includes a wide spectrum of practices, not all of which are tolerated at the same time.

Human nature may even play a large part in generating them for, if you survey history, you will commonly find that homosexuality and the use of children for sex more often occurs when a people has become overpopulated, making them ways to limit reproduction.

That doesn't mean they have to be given free reign, as there are other ways of limiting reproduction, too; such as abstinence, celibacy and the use of prophylactics. But it does mean that, in one respect, he was right: you can expect to find them occurring again and again in human nature.

Another thing I discovered in meeting my fellow sex offenders is that our families are very similar—as dysfunctional as they can be. If the biological purpose of the family is to reproduce the human race and then rear its children until they can maintain themselves, that is what it means to say there is a functional family.

If you have a dysfunctional one, where the parents are so problem-ridden as to cause their children to come out crazy after living with them, that is a dysfunctional family, and that is what all of us had.

Our mothers, in particular, were so very much like each other that we joked among ourselves that any of us could get on a pay phone with someone else's mother and probably not even notice the difference.

Nor, probably, would she.

Tremendously possessive, our mothers smothered us and in the process sought to devour us. Always treating us as if we were children, they stunted our growth by always making an excuse for us whenever we failed. And that made me wonder just how safe our mothers would be if we got involved with them again when we got out—as most such men did, for no one else would take them.

The sanest thing to do with convicted sex offenders when they get out of prison is to place them in a common shelter with appropriate supervision. The Colorado Department of Public Safety did this and made a study afterwards, to see how the men did while there. Across the board, they found that those who lived in such settings had a far lower rate of re-offense than others living with their families. (2004 Shared Living Arrangements Report, Colorado Department of Public Safety.)

Citizens object, for public safety reasons, when homes of this kind are proposed. But if located away from residential neighborhoods, perhaps in an industrial part of the city, or on its far edges, there is no reason why more facilities of this type could not be established, giving the community a far greater degree of safety than it has now.

To Heal or To Punish?

When my request for further psychotherapy was approved, I was given a prison psychologist with whom I'd meet each Monday for one hour. To prepare for those sessions, I had the guards lock me in my cell the day beforehand, so I could have the time and the privacy to search within myself for anything I wanted to bring up. And quietly weep, if I needed to do so, for there were a lot of tears inside me.

I was amazed as I searched my memories to find so many injuries buried there: like the fact that my father had rejected me as a child because I didn't like football or baseball like he did. I liked swimming and, when I got into my teens, I'd even begun working-out at a gym, but those activities weren't good enough to earn his acceptance. That hurt me, even then.

Then there was my mother, and all those times when she'd treated me like no more than a toy she took with her, wherever she went: often leaving me on a sofa with nothing to do, while she gossiped with friends or relatives she visited in another room. I must have spent half my childhood sleeping out of boredom.

What I soon realized was that, like all sex offenders, I'd never really had any sense of self—of being a person whose faith in himself, alone, was adequate to meet the challenges that life presents.

Lacking that, I had no self-respect and, without self-respect, no respect for anyone else. So I lived a life that disrespected me, I traveled in its gutters instead of in its heavens, unconsciously believing that I didn't deserve the heavens because I'd never been treated as someone who did.

The lesson that leaves us with is that, if you want your child to become a moral person, you begin by respecting him or her as a person: as a human being possessed with whatever their unique talents might be. You encourage the genius given to them by their nature. You don't try to make your child into your reflection but into their own.

I told my doctor that the reason I wanted to see him was because I wanted to learn why I had molested my daughter. Fearful that I might be prosecuted further if I said anything about any other acts I had committed, I did what everyone else did in prison and never mentioned them. Had I done otherwise, they would have been reported and I might have had to face additional charges.

Some say that not talking about them is harmful, as it doesn't get all of the person's problems addressed. In a case handed down in the United States just before the time of this writing (*McKune v. Lile*), the Supreme

Court said much the same thing. Under its ruling, states were given permission to make a prisoner's confinement even harsher if he wouldn't tell his keepers about crimes for which he had not yet been caught. But doctors I know who conduct group therapy programs outside of prison, which often include men still awaiting trial—men who *can't* talk about their crimes, on the advice of their attorneys—say that such men are still dealing with their problems just by being in the group. "They hear what we're saying and they know if it applies to them."

Perhaps what the defense bar still hasn't succeeded in communicating to the bench is that, unlike tent revival meetings, where a sinner cannot be forgiven unless he loudly proclaims all his sins to others, psychotherapy is a different kind of process altogether. What is necessary in psychotherapy is that you face the truth about yourself, to yourself. It is the individual who has to do the work, not the doctor. Whether the patient tells the doctor about something or not, the patient still knows what that something is and is working on it, even when confining the discussion only to those things which can safely be discussed.

As I wrote, in part, to *The New York Times* reporter who covered that United States Supreme Court case:

> For all the importance that an honest admission has, speaking out of my own experience I say that it doesn't necessarily have to be made to a person who will prosecute you for it…
>
> There are those who, as in *Lile*, believe…one can only find redemption by self-rejection, while there are others…who believe one can only find redemption by accepting one's self as their life does: as a work still in progress, and then progressing it.
>
> *—E-mail to Linda Greenhouse dated*
> *January 11, 2002*

Who is going to risk being given another prison sentence when they haven't even finished the one they already have, just to fill in the record?

To meet this challenge, some prosecutors are now choosing not to press charges for disclosures made by prisoners in prison therapy programs.

They are issuing what are called *waivers* from further prosecution for anything admitted in counseling, and that is helping a lot of men to get the help they need without having to fear more jail time for doing so.

The only problem is that further criminal prosecution isn't the only threat that an admitted offender now faces in some states. Since at least the early nineties in the United States, new laws now require some sex offenders to be committed to mental hospitals after their imprisonment if they admit too much, keeping them locked up even longer. As a result, some defense attorneys are warning their clients that freedom from criminal prosecution isn't enough and, so far as this writer knows, no prosecutor yet has waived both further prosecution *and* post-imprisonment civil commitment, moving us right back to where we started: offenders—fearful of no end to being kept locked up—are not willing to divulge any other crimes than the ones for which they've been convicted.

And some won't even choose to see a doctor out of fear they would be prosecuted for saying anything.

This nation needs to make a choice as to whether we are evil or ill. If evil, and no more than that, prison alone, for life, is all that is called for. But if driven to do evil by forces we never chose, you get the person treated so he can have his life back. To punish a person for having mental problems hasn't been done since the Dark Ages.

The point is made best by one of the letters I received from convicted sex offenders who write me from all over the nation now. It came from a person who raped his three-year old brother; one of the worst crimes it is possible to imagine.

But he is only fourten years old and hasn't a clue as to why he did this. Can we possibly be so barbaric that we would say punishment alone is all he needs?

Are we so lacking in charity for a child driven by evil forces to do a deed like this that we will not help him get his mental health back? If we, as a people, cannot see those who obviously need treatment as deserving of the same, than *we* are spiritually ill, for we have lost our connection to the human heart.

Blame and Responsibility

My doctor was no fool, by the way. He was a prison psychologist, accustomed to facing men who lied to him every day. I doubt that I really had to tell him there might have been other offenses. As a result, by the end of a year of our meeting together, he had some answers for me.

"While it's clear that your father never molested you, there's no question but that he was, shall we say, 'overly-affectionate.' And that it was your mother who was the problem."

I recall that the doctor said I should hate her "as she was the one who messed you up."

He wasn't the first doctor who had said so. While I was in treatment and my case was waiting to be heard, another doctor had said the same thing.

But as I told this doctor, I just didn't think that hating my mother was the answer.

"I know too much about her own background to do that. That she damaged me I do not doubt. But that she alone did so is untrue as she, in turn, had been damaged by those who raised her who, in turn, had been damaged by others, and so on, making it merely an act of choice to say we shall blame her, as if none of these others had ever existed. All of them damaged me."

Blame is just a legal term, used by courts to determine who is going to pay the injured party, in cash or through involuntary servitude as a prisoner of the state. It has nothing to do with healing, where we can identify the source of the damage so that it can be removed.

Other people who look like the creator of the damage are only carriers of a damaging process that moves through them. While they can—and should—be held accountable for letting it come through, we can't accurately call anyone it's real creator because there is no such individual. There is just life, and in life sometimes people get hurt: earthquakes happen and people get injured by them. Emotional earthquakes happen, too, and that's what sometimes makes a parent fail. You can't blame anyone for having an emotional earthquake. The best you can do is build them back up so they don't have another.

In that respect, the view expressed by our criminal law—that the offender, alone, is to blame for having become an offender—is like blaming a storm on itself, without including the climate that produced it. In the victim's pain, he or she wants vengeance, and who can fault them? All they can see is the offender himself, not all of the others who may go back for generations in the forming of that offender. And so the victims cry out of their pain, "Punish him!"

But law should have more vision than that and, instead of merely punishing, it should also seek to confine the offender in prison until he is healed, and see that he gets an opportunity to be healed: that would be wisdom, which we have a right to demand of the law.

The doctor stared at me in wonder, and with a wry grin on his face said, "You're crazy, did you know that? You're as crazy as Charles Manson."

I wanted additional answers, so the following week I sent in a request for something called transpersonal counseling, which would look not only at my mind but into my spirit itself. I now suspected that my spirit had been damaged, too, and needed to be fixed if I was ever to have a life that was under my control. When I received a reply that this kind of counseling wasn't available in any of the prison's psychology programs I turned, instead, to where it could be found: in the Chaplain's Office.

Statistical findings since that time may suggest that I was wise to do so as it now turns out that offenders who have had therapy do no better than those who had none. Comparing members of both groups it was found that, after twelve years, one out of every five men in both groups re-offends. (Hanson, Broom and Stephenson, 2004.) Those who do and do not receive therapy do just as well.

What could be added that would make a meaningful difference? I was about to find out.

* * *

How to Protect Your Children

1. Don't let anyone try to convince you that all we have to do to stop sex offenders is have them castrated when the offender's problem isn't in his groin but in his mind.

2. Don't let anyone try and tell you that sex offending can't be "cured" unless they also admit that it can be managed by the offender given training to do so.

3. Don't let anyone convince you that convicted offenders meeting in approved maintenance groups will only waste their time trying to figure out ways to find more victims. If you really have doubts about such a group, phone your local police and have them look into it for you.

4. Don't believe that convicted sex offenders are safer if they are living alone or with their families instead of in an approved group shelter program. Urge your members of Congress and the state legislature to create such programs.

5. Tell your child never to let any stranger into your home, no matter what government agency they claim to represent.

6. Tell your children never to go off alone with anyone unless it is someone you know, too, and know where they are going and how they can be reached there.

7. Give them a cell phone already programmed to dial 911 or your own cell phone's number at the touch of a button whenever they are away from you.

*   *   *

Questions to Consider

1. Is your own sex drive an urge or a deliberate choice?

2. If you were a convicted sex offender, would you admit to every crime you committed?

3. Is the parent who damages his child to be blamed for how that child turns out? Or is there a line somewhere, when we can say he is excused and only his child is accountable? If so, when does that line begin to exist?

Chapter Six

A God for Sex Offenders

Can religion 'save' a sex offender? One of the convicted predators I met in prison—who had now become a very devout Catholic—told me that he knew he would never offend again when he got out because "Jesus" would save him.

I question whether we have the right to make that His job. In recovery literature, there's an anonymous saying I like much better: "*Without God, I can't. Without me, God won't.*" Recovery requires a partnership, not God acting as Santa Claus.

Sunday school religion won't get you there; it is only a start. What it usually takes is a divorce, or at least a separation, from the God of your childhood until you grow up enough to accept a more mature relationship.

Tragedy often plays a useful part, for only through tragedy will most of us face how utterly powerless we really are and either accept it and heal into that partnership, or continue to suffer.

The world is not a 'nice' place. Every day children are killed here: whether by war, famine, natural disaster, infanticide or accidents. We Americans, in particular, don't like to think that, sheltered as we have been for most of our history by oceans on either side that have kept the rest of the world away from us. In Europe, Africa and Asia, as well as Latin America, people haven't had such moats. The result is that they know, first hand, how brutal life can be as their neighbors have often taught them. We, on the other hand, persist in the naïve believe that 'bad' things aren't supposed to happen here and must be 'mistakes.'

That is not correct: Life is both good and bad; that is how it comes. And at times the bad can be absolutely awful.

That is when many of us get the chance to accept a version of God that has been revered in the Eastern part of the world for centuries: one that destroys as well as creates. The Hebrew prophet Isaiah saw this, and told everyone.

"Behold," he quotes God as saying, in Isaiah 45:6-7, "I am the Lord, and there is none else...I make peace *and create evil:* I the Lord do all these things." (The Holy Bible, King James Version, italics added for emphasis.)

There is only one source. And we will never understand it. All we can do is accept it and fashion a way to work with it. Most people won't. I was one of the lucky ones: I had no choice but to accept it as it had already made the terms of my continued life unmistakably clear: either I grew up, spiritually, or it would kill me.

I was fortunate. A full-time Jewish chaplain had just been added to the staff of our institution and I seized that opportunity to place myself under his teaching. In his forties and thin as a rail, with a small prayer cap always worn on top of his head, he squinted at me from behind rimless eyeglasses as I told him, "I'd like to study Jewish Mysticism," the grown-up's version of religion.

His reply was unconditional. "I don't teach Jewish Mysticism."

I nodded that I understood, for mysticism—in any religion—doesn't just deal with knowing about the Almighty, but directly experiencing it in your life as real as anything else, which is not a light thing to take on.

Seeing the determined look on my face he added, "But I'll tell you what I will do. If you will let me teach you the fundamentals of our religion, after I'm done—if you still want to study 'Jewish Mysticism'—I'll get you some scholarly books on the subject and you can study it yourself."

He warned me that 'mysticism'—and mystic experiences—can be very taxing. "Our state mental hospitals," he cautioned me, "are full of 'Great Jewish Mystics' and I don't want you to become another one. But if you have your fundamentals down and ever get lost out there, at least you'll have a safety net to fall back on."

That seemed perfectly reasonable so I accepted his conditions. Whenever I wasn't working at a prison-assigned job, I studied the materials he gave me to use in my cell and then went to see him once each week to discuss them.

A Yeshiva Behind Bars

We began with a basic primer, and then went on to study the Holy Scriptures (what non-Jews call "The Old Testament"). Under his guidance, what I found repeatedly was a *call* within them from a parent who ached for the return of a child who called back that it was lost. What I came to see is that humanity needs God to find itself, just as much as God needs humanity to know itself.

When I learned enough Hebrew to do so, I went on to study Torah, the sacred writings of our people as expressed through the first five books of the Old Testament. The word *torah* means "plan" and its central concept is that there is a plan for our lives and that Torah contains that plan in symbolic form.

Originally written on long sections of sheepskin called *sedras*, one section is read every week on the Sabbath to mirror the changing phases of the Moon that mirror the changing phases of our lives. All of these *sedras* were sewn together, end-upon-end, and then suspended between two long spools upon which they could be rolled. Each week, when Torah is brought out, it is unrolled, just like our destiny.

Collectively, the story it tells is one of separation and reconciliation: creation, fall from grace, a life that is flooded and then recovers, only to wind up becoming enslaved before one's worthiness is tested and one's Promised Land is finally found.

It gives us our plan, if we will accept it. Most don't and, after a childhood in Eden, get lost in the world as casualties of ambition, wealth and love that goes bad.

The Rabbi was very specific about that enslavement. "It wasn't just to Egypt," he insisted, referring to the story found in The Book of Exodus. "It's enslavement to the *world*. You can get just as enslaved today by living a life so secular that it doesn't include any lasting values. Torah tells us that our people came to be so dominated by the world of their time that they couldn't even *remember* the name of their God."

Embarrassed, I cleared my throat.

We went beyond Judaism, into the time before there was a Judaism, back before the time of Moses. It can be found in the Book of Genesis, where one reads of a people called the *Ha-biru* (later known as Hebrews) which means those from "the other side" of the city walls, the peoples of the Sinai Desert who at one time worshipped a Goddess named Sin (pronounced *Seen*).

It is said that her symbol was The Moon for, just like life, the Moon is always changing on its surface while its wholeness remains constant. She was said to have presided over her holy desert in which they lived, from atop her sacred mountain where she watched them dance out their lives below. Hence, both were named after her: Mount *Sin*-ai and the *Sin*-ai Desert.

Her legacy remains today in the Jewish Mystical notion of the *Shekinah*, or Bride of God, the feminine side of the Godhead, to whom a glass of wine is raised—just like one does at weddings—on every sabbath coinciding with the New Moon. Every Jewish man is potentially her groom and every Jewish woman represents The Bride of God. In Judaism, even sex is sacred.

That's when the Rabbi directed his teaching to my case.

"Tell me," he said, leaning back in his chair, "do you have any idea why we consecrate our allegiance to God by placing the Mark of Circumcision on *that* particular part of the human body?

"No," I said, completely puzzled. I'd never thought about it before.

"Well," he responded, "think about it. I mean, we could have placed such a mark elsewhere, by notching our ears, or nose, as other peoples have done. Why do you think we chose to make that mark on the *penis*?"

I squirmed in my seat as I said that I couldn't imagine a reason why. Then he gave me the answer. "We put it there," he told me sternly, "to remind ourselves that *all* of our urges must be submitted to the Will of God—even *that* one."

A wall of shame fell over me. I had not just sinned against the law, but against the Giver of Law.

That night, alone in my cell, with the moon as my only witness through the barred window, I got down on my knees, bowed my head and made my confession.

"Aveinu malkeno," I began aloud, in Hebrew.

I was offering what is called *The Midnight Prayer*: one that cannot be heard until one reaches the midnight of their life as it cannot be spoken until it is midnight in one's soul.

"My father, my king: forgive me, for I have *offended* Thee…"

There is a Plan.

Conversations with Divinity

True to his word, once I'd satisfied him that I'd mastered all of Judaism's essentials, the Rabbi supplied me with several of the finest works on Jewish Mysticism and I spent the balance of my tutorial under him in studying them. My conclusions are my own, however, and should not be taken as his, for the essence of mysticism is what it is for you only (something every religious fanatic either forgets or never understands).

At the same time, I also studied Eastern Mysticism and, out of studying both, what I learned is not only that there is a Plan for our lives, but that we help shape it whether we know it or not. While we are given the *conditions* of our lives, such as where we are born and who our parents are, *how* we use those conditions is up to us, as are its effects.

The same idea is found in the ancient philosophies and religions of India and China, as I discovered when I also studied a copy of the *I Ching* that I ordered in prison from its publisher.

Doing Time with the *I Ching*

Originally transmitted only by memory, 3000 years ago the work was first written down by a prisoner. Later known as King Wen, he had led a revolt against the ruling dynasty in China. Captured by his enemies, he was locked up and held for ransom. It was during his imprisonment that he produced the first written version of this work that had previously been known, just like the stories of Torah, only through oral recitation by great sages.

When his son later rescued him, they completed the revolution and founded what became known as the Chou Dynasty. The *I Ching* became the official bible of their kingdom. When the great Chinese philosopher, Confucius, added further explanations to King Wen's writings, the work went on to become the most revered book in Chinese literature, just as the written Torah did with the ancient Hebrews.

Much like Torah, the *I Ching* also issues a call: to live a balanced life. Just as Torah tells of how the Hebrews went from victory to defeat over and over again as they made their way across the Sinai, the *I Ching* tells us that it is the normal course of our lives to be filled and then emptied repeatedly, like a lake. When I finally grasped this, it totally changed the way I saw the world. That's when my recovery took root.

Unlike the fairy-tale version of life, where everyone lives "happily ever after," the *I Ching* paints a version of life that is more like war, which is closer to the mark in a world where every species in it—including ours—struggles endlessly for survival. In this work, just as in life, there is no final peace, only brief moments of rest, when one is not being besieged.

More importantly, what it teaches us is how *not* to besiege ourselves. It tells us that, every time we come to have too much of anything, loss always results. We trigger it by overloading ourselves. By *not* seeking so much of everything we have the ability to modulate our lives and make them more peaceful.

Think of life as a meal at a restaurant. If you want a grand feast, you certainly can have one. But the price will be steep. Or, you can have a more modest meal, and the price will be reasonable.

It's up to us. We already are the co-creators of our lives, whether we know it or not. We can choose *not* to stuff ourselves and thereby avoid life's heartburns.

Most of us don't: we stuff ourselves with too much food, or too much sex or too much money or too much liquor or too much of anything and then we complain about feeling ill afterwards, as if it was the restaurant's fault.

The restaurant only served what you asked for!

And so we come to sex. You can have as much as you want, of any kind that you want. The world is a cafeteria and if it isn't available at this spot in the line, go further down and you'll find it there.

And it will always have a cost. Even if you sneak out the door and get away without paying it, there is still a cost, it's a just a different kind of cost. You can't go back to that cafeteria again. Or its owners may come after you.

All life is created in opposites. We get what we want and its cost. For every sunrise, there is a sunset and for every mountain a valley. One can no more have 'good' without 'bad' than one can breathe in without breathing out.

If you go after forbidden sex, the cost is even higher.

It might be jail. It might be a sexually-transmitted disease. It might be the fear of jail, so great that you'd always be on the run, always worried that, someday, they might catch you. It might be revenge, cruelly taken by someone on behalf of the person you had molested. I knew someone like that: a very successful child molester. Until police found him lying in his apartment with the back of his head blown off.

It isn't just a matter of what the *law* says. Any reasonably intelligent person can figure out a way to break the law without getting caught, at least for awhile, or go live in some other country where the laws aren't so strict. But what this teaching was telling me is that there is *another* law, like gravity: so sewn into the very fabric of life that, no matter where I ran and what I did, it would be impossible for me to keep from experiencing it because, while you are eating with one hand, you are writing up the bill with the other!

Everything has consequences, and those consequences will occur. All we can change is *where* they will find us, not whether. We're not looking at just some penal code. We're looking at what the ancient Chinese appropriately called *The Statutes of Heaven*.

"Fear of the Lord," the Rabbi taught me, "is the beginning of wisdom."

No wonder I wound up being sent to prison! I had invoked it by the kind of life I had lived. I could no more harm another without harming myself than I could take a hammer and hit my own toe without feeling pain. The victim of an act of sexual abuse isn't the only one injured by it— *so is the offender*. The sooner the offender realizes this, the sooner he will stop offending.

The pharaoh of sexual addiction had just met its Moses.

Completing Creation

I went to the prison library and brought books back to my cell about other men's imprisonments, in other lands and at other times, so that I could better understand my own. For imprisonment, no matter when it is and where it is, always has something about it at its core that makes it uniformly the same, as if one has entered a timeless brotherhood that cuts right across centuries and civilizations and somehow unites them.

I read about Japanese internment camps in the Pacific. I read Solzhenitsyns' massive work, *The Gulag Archipelago*, which described the brutality of the former Soviet Union's prison camps in Siberia during the 1930's and 1940's. I read about Nazi concentration camps and the experiences of Jews who had lived in them during World War II. All of these books taught me something.

Solzhenitsyn wrote that evil has what he called a *threshold magnitude*— a point which, once passed, makes it impossible for a person to ever come back to the human campfire because he has gone so far into the darkness that there isn't time enough in a human life to make the return journey.

I wondered, in fear, if this might apply to me. I realized, however, that while a person might commit an act so evil that they would never be welcome back in mainstream society, he could still come back from evil and live a better life, even if outside of society or on its margins. Anyone can redeem himself, if he wants to do so enough.

I read Elie Wiesel's poignant story of the time when everyone in his Nazi concentration camp was made to silently witness the hanging of three of its members suspected of being saboteurs, one of whom was only a child.

He tells us that members of the SS placed a noose around the little boy's neck just like they had done with the others. The two adults died instantly, when their necks snapped from the weight of their body's being hung but, as the child was small, his death was not instant and he was left, suspended and wiggling like a fish on dry land, while everyone else in the camp was forced to witness it. He was still dying when all the other prisoners were made to march past him and look into his face.

A man in the crowd who could take it no more hissed out bitterly to Wiesel, "Where is God? Where is He?"

Wiesel heard an answer within himself: "Here…hanging on this gallows…"

He could have also said *and in the Nazis who hung him.* For—"Behold," proclaims God, in *Isaiah* 45:6-7, "both good *and evil* do I create."

God is in *all* beings: in the child who is molested; in the man who molests him; in the policeman who arrests him; in the judge who sentences him, and in the warden who confines him. God permits everything, leaving it to us to complete creation by establishing limits and morals.

I had to limit myself from now on; that was clearly my task if I really wanted to repair the damage that had been done to my spirit many years before by a mother who hated sex and several other people who only knew its destructive side.

This was my calling and I now accepted it. Almost as if in response, I was given the means to do so and entered the Partnership.

The Hungry Ghost

I was transferred to work as a clerk-typist at a Southern California prison treatment center for drug addicts, strange as that may sound. But something awaited me there that I couldn't get anyplace else and my prison counselors obviously knew I needed it: the means by which we can control our addiction to anything. It was called Relapse Prevention Training.

With lush gardens and beautiful trees planted all over its gently rolling grounds, it was a nicer place to be than in a regular prison's yard, that was for sure. As a matter of fact, the place looked more like a private convalescent center (which it once had been) than a prison, although there was now a chain-link fence around its perimeter, where guard towers holding correctional officers looked down on us—just to make certain that no one escaped from *Shangri-la.*

Instead of cells, however, we lived in dormitories of one-hundred men each. Because the addicts were only held here for nine months before being released, the atmosphere was far more relaxed than a regular penal institution.

Not to say that there wasn't any violence. Five inmates were placed in The Hole one time on suspicion of something or another. When investigating officers found that the youngest among them had absolutely nothing to do with whatever the others had been up to, they cut him loose and returned him to the yard. But among narcotics addicts, the only way one man gets released while others continue to be held is through his being a snitch and telling on the others, which is considered unforgivable. As a result, on his first day back on the yard, they stabbed him.

You might say that it was like the Betty Ford Clinic—with *The Sopranos* there.

The men received counseling, took classes in addiction and received specialized training in how to overcome those self-destructive habits that continually led to their undoing. Upon release, they were kept under supervision in the community for several years, but automatically returned for another nine months if they failed to stay clean.

I met a number who had been back, repeatedly. They reminded me of *The Hungry Ghost*—a creature spoken of in Buddhism who is perpetually driven by a thirst he cannot fill, as what he seeks to nourish it with is, like salt water, the very thing that causes his thirst. As I listened to the men describe their cravings, I began to understand that my addiction to sex was no different than theirs to drugs. They craved intoxication, just as I did. Like them, what I craved kept me so locked in its embrace that it finally ruled my life at the expense of anything else—job, family, career, everything. I realized then that whatever helped an alcoholic or addict kick his habit might also help me kick mine, after all.

I recalled that book that I had browsed through while at an earlier prison, published by Alcoholics Anonymous, that set forth a twelve-step program used successfully by thousands of former compulsive drinkers. Narcotics therapists were now using similar methods and I saw no reason why I could not do so, too.

As I watched the men around me come and go (and, so often, return), I listened as they told of their dysfunctional families, whose members actually seemed to have driven these men to fail, who seemed to need to have them fail so they didn't have to face their own enormous problems. It sounded very much like my family. I, too, had failed repeatedly and my parents had always had an excuse ready for me. As a result, I continued to fail.

"Enablers," such people are called in the addiction field. Enablers are addicted to someone else's always remaining an addict, so that they're always needed by him. I've since come to know of a few politicians and community alarmists who are the same way toward sex offenders: doing everything they can to make sure we fail, by stirring so much resentment up about us in the community as to make it impossible for us to come back. Instead, they would have us stay banished—just outside of the community—so they can continue to represent themselves to the community as "the only one who can save you."

It isn't that the addict isn't given *love* by his family. It's that the love given isn't a *healthy* love. It was what Author John Bradshaw calls a *toxic* love, one that poisons its recipient. Instead of helping him to grow, it stunts him.

Like narcotics addicts, alcoholics, and even people who always seem to go from one abusive emotional relationship to another, most sex offenders come from a background where they've been 'cued' to always injure themselves. Raised in a destructive family setting, many of us—both perpetrators and victims (and how often we both come from the same kind of family)—unconsciously follow paths that lead only to our being abused. We follow cues we were given in childhood by the families who raised us.

It is a mental conditioning we can only escape by leaving what best-selling Author Pia Mellody terms *the family trance*. That means living our life apart from such families.

That was the work that had to be done if we were to leave prison and never come back. Very few men in the nation's prisons are ready to do so when they get out and, as a result, most keep returning to prisons across the country that are kept in business by not having treatment programs like this one.

Relapse Prevention

At the core of the institution's treatment for addicts was the teaching that, if you were simply honest enough with yourself to admit that you're tempted by certain situations, you could avoid putting yourself in them. For example, if you drink every time that you are depressed, whenever you find yourself beginning to feel low, you give yourself some other way to deal with it, such as giving yourself some ice cream or a candy bar, or calling someone from your Alcoholics Anonymous group to help you get past that low.

You don't foolishly tempt yourself by deliberately putting yourself near the things that your addiction craves, like the person who claims to be a recovering alcoholic but purchases a bottle of whisky *just to have in the house in case guests come over.*

Such a person isn't concerned about guests: he's just trying to see how close he can get to the edge of the wagon before he falls off of it.

In the case of a child molester, he might decide to live in a suburban neighborhood full of children, or right next door to a school. He might even involve himself in a youth group. If he is a rapist, he might take up jogging and run along the same trails that women use.

To prevent this, one learns to look back and remember the sequence of events that always led up to their offending—in what was called our offense cycle—and identify each of those things that always began it: our so-called triggering mechanisms.

Were we depressed? Fatigued? Confused? So intoxicated with success that we felt that we could have *anything* now?

What kind of targets tempted us? Young boys, little girls on the edge of adolescence, women who look sad? Only the most ruthless self-honesty works here and the deeper we probe, the stronger we become in avoiding our own destructive urges. Ultimately, we'd know them all, like the FBI knows its Public Enemies, for these are ours.

I had encouragement from the institution; they were kind enough to have a gun tower in my yard. Every time I went outside of my dormitory I saw it looking down at me. The message it seemed to be sending was very clear: that if, when I got out, I went back to living the same old way that

I had lived before I came to prison, it was as certain as tomorrow's sunrise that I would come back to prison and find that same old gun tower looking down on me once again.

I could count on it. My counselors even told me so when I mentioned it to them. "We're glad you noticed," they said.

I had other encouragement, too. One of the correctional officers under whom I worked decided to invest in me. Every week, on my day off from work, he allowed me to meet with him in his office, where we discussed all the things that might tempt me to relapse once I was released from prison, and how I might sidestep them. We developed what are called *Escape Strategies* that I could use, which would allow me to immediately get away from any situation that threatened me with temptation.

Knowing that it might not always be possible to get away from some situations immediately, we went further and developed what are called *Coping Strategies*, designed to allow me to handle threatening situations responsibly until I could escape from them.

Week by week we went over my record, and as we did so what I finally found was that the thing that caused me to engage in my whole addictive process was anger within me for even daring to believe that I could ever succeed in life. It was if some Evil Queen lived deeply within me and demanded to know how I could possibly dare to believe that I was her king.

Again and again, I wilted in her mental presence and engaged in self-destructive habits that 'proved' I wasn't worthy to be anybody's king. I found her origin within my family. Its members were all angry at life and angry at themselves. Rather than take responsibility for having permitted others to abuse them, they lived out their lives as if each of them were the lead singer in a tragic opera, singing for the world's pity and getting only their own.

It was the *family game* and it rapidly became clear that my best interests lay in staying free of it. As one of my counselors warned me in a moment of total honesty, just before I was released from prison, "Look out: you've changed, they haven't."

By the time that Release Day approached, I was holding one of the highest jobs that an inmate could have in prison, working for one of the Acting Wardens as his chief clerk. Like Joseph, I stood at Pharaoh's right hand. By having chosen that myth at the very beginning of my imprisonment, it appears that I had activated its power in my life.

And so it happened that, five years and two months after I had walked in, I left prison and caught a bus and went back to L.A., checking myself in to a quiet, family-run hotel I knew of just at the base of the Hollywood Hills.

That evening at sunset I stood at the bottom of the hill that had repeatedly come to me in a vision when my imprisonment had first begun and I went up to the temple on top. The Power of my Life had kept its promise and I thanked it for having done so.

I had some answers now.

*   *   *

How to Protect Your Children

1. Teach your children that their job is to take care of their lives by being careful where they go and with whom they travel.

2. Teach them the truth about life: that it can be dangerous, and we *all* have the task of living carefully. We cannot live as if nothing can happen to us.

3. Teach them not to be the first to try anything they haven't learned about fully, such as cigarettes with strange smells, drugs and so-called "thriller" drinks; some young people have been killed by these.

4. Teach your children that everything we do has consequences that cannot be avoided, so they must act carefully and with good sense.

5. Set limits to what they do, how late they can stay out, and where they can go and enforce those limits. Right now, you are their Guard Tower.

6. Don't excuse them when they fail to stay within the limits you have set. Hold them accountable or their life will do so, the hard way.

7. Don't be an absent parent, not home on the weekends when your kids are going out, or at least have a way they can reach you, wherever you are.

8. Teach them that sex is not a toy we are given, but a power that is sacred. Teach them to live modestly as there really is such a thing as going 'too far.' People don't come back from there.

9. Teach them that fear of the Lord—no matter how you define that term—is the beginning of wisdom, so they may stay protected by it and not live as a slave.

*   *   *

Questions to Consider

1. Can a person convicted of a sex offense return to society and become a member again?

2. Are there some who should not come back, but live in their own colonies, distant from the community?

3. Should our sex offender registration laws also tell you if the sex offender has had any counseling or treatment programs?

4. Should our sex offender registration laws also tell you the method that the offender used to find his victims, so you could make sure he isn't using them again?

5. What would the sex offender's life look like, if it were described as a journey?

Chapter Seven

Dancing with a Higher Power

Homecoming

The first morning I was back, my mother came by and took me to brunch. Urging me to name my favorite restaurant, she drove me right over there.

"Have anything you want," she said cheerily, as soon as we were seated.

Relaxing in the embrace of her good will, I ordered my favorite sandwich and was so relieved that I wasn't going to have to get into a long, drawn-out discussion about my offense. But the moment my sandwich arrived, that illusion was shattered. As I opened my mouth to take that first delicious bite, she struck:

"*Why* did you do it?"

I was home again.

Setting the sandwich back down on my plate, I replied: "The doctors said it was *your* fault."

She snorted at the notion. "Doctors! What do *they* know?"

"Do you still take your high-blood pressure medication?"

Hurriedly, she opened her purse and peered inside, to make certain she'd brought along her pills. When she looked up again, she saw me smiling at her mischievously and became embarrassed.

Then she struck again. "You can't come up to the house, you know. I don't want you there."

Nervously folding her hands repeatedly, she quickly amended that to insist it was the fault of other relatives—*they* didn't want me there.

"We'll have lunch again," she assured me, "once each month." Then she quickly reached inside her purse and gave me a folded check with enough money to live on, at least modestly, for my first year back. "Welcome home."

Additional checks would follow if I stayed away.

This was not the time to quarrel with her or force my presence on anyone. It made it lonely for me not to be around my family, especially on holidays, but all things considered it was probably a blessing. At least I wouldn't become one of those taken off parole and sent back to prison because '*the family complained that he made too many problems.*' I knew that I could find other emotional resources, and that's what I concentrated on doing.

Under my state's rules, I would be under the supervision of a parole agent for three years and I went to report in to him, as required, the first day of the following week.

I was surprised by how long I was kept waiting in the reception area when I got there, but I figured it was his day to do with me as he wanted, and this was just part of it.

When I was finally shown back to his office, the first thing I noticed was that he was glaring at me from his side of the desk, so I stopped in his doorway rather than come in any further.

He said: "We understand you intend to kidnap your daughter and take her to South America!"

It didn't take much to figure out who would have concocted a story like that one. Prior to being released on parole, authorities routinely interview a prisoner's family and it was the kind of hysterical claim that only my mother could have made, so I simply nodded and said, "Well, I'll tell you. On Saturday, I had lunch with my mother. At the end of the meal, she gave me this."

Reaching into my shirt pocket, I took out her check and handed it to him. His eyes blinked when he saw the amount—more than enough to go to South America—which told him that if I had meant to go there I would have already left.

As he silently passed it back to me I said, "If those allegations were true, I don't think I'd be here right now, do you?"

He laughed to himself heartily and said, "Well, you know how it is: we hear all kinds of *bull-shit* and just gotta' check it out. Come on in, Goldenflame. I'm sure we're going to have a very positive relationship. *Congratulations* on reporting in on-time!"

We got on fine, from that moment. He had his rules, and I accepted them:

—No drugs

—No drinking

—No contact with my ex-wife or her family

—Not being alone with any child under fourteen years of age

—Registering the location of my residence with police, and

—Seeing an approved psychotherapist during my first year back.

Since I wouldn't be totally free again until I had completed my parole, completing it was the only thing that mattered to me. If I'd learned anything from all of the accounts that other men had told me at my last facility, the one thing that made some fail more than any other was their own unwillingness to make success at parole their primary goal.

To be even more certain that I would complete parole without being taken back to prison—which parole is authorized to do if you fail to satisfy your officer—in addition to the rules that he gave me, I added four more of my own. I'd recommend them to anybody when they get out of prison:

- **Be off the streets by 10:00 PM on weekends,** so as not to be around if any trouble breaks out.

- **Avoid any problem area,** for the same reason, and don't do anything to attract the attention of police.

- **When you have an appointment to meet with your parole agent, get there on time and be willing to wait—the rest of the day if necessary—without complaining about it.**

- **Treat your parole agent with respect and you'll be given the same.** Upon his arrival in my room, I always gave him the best chair to sit in, while I sat on the sofa-bed. At the end of each visit, I always escorted him back out to his car and politely waited until he left before going on my way. He returned my courtesies by doing such things as always calling before coming to my house, something that he certainly wasn't required to do.

Right before I got out of prison, my last counselor had given me the best advice as to how to succeed on parole. "Just don't forget," she said, "that *you're still in custody*. When you first came in, we kept you behind high walls. During parole, you'll be kept behind *rules*. Treat them as your walls and you'll never have any trouble."

I did as she said and it worked.

Where Should a Sex Offender Live?

I wanted a quiet place to live so there wouldn't be any problems. I had already heard too many stories about halfway houses where everyone was taken back to prison because of the misconduct of a few. I intended to avoid them.

Jewish facilities were out of the question. Just before my training with the Rabbi ended, he took me aside and explained that, because our people were family-oriented, they probably wouldn't want me around, and I accepted that. By looking through a local newspaper I located a rooming house run by a Buddhist organization and went down there and rented a room that very day.

My fellow tenants would be Buddhist monks and I wouldn't have enough privacy to tempt me into getting into any improper activities. I also knew that my parole agent would like my being there, as it was a clean, quiet and respectable place, and that was important too.

I was right. The first day he came over to see the place, he almost hit his head on the huge bronze gong at the base of the stairs, but he was impressed.

"It's not," he confessed, "what I'm used to seeing when I call on parolees."

Good. That's how I wanted it to stay.

I had to register my address with the police as a convicted sex offender. It was before *Megan's Law*, so I'd been told that my registration would never be made public, but I had my doubts. I felt certain that anyone who wanted to do so could hire a private detective to do a background check and find out if a person was on this list or not. For that same reason, I figured it probably could also be discovered by any employer with a good job to offer, or a significant promotion later, and I didn't like the limit that seemed to place on me.

I was also uncomfortable with it on a deeper level. A law requiring registration of a whole class of citizens bothered me. It brought back unpleasant memories from my childhood, of muted conversations between relatives in the other room, speaking of Nazi Germany where all of our people had been registered just before being rounded up and made to live in secluded parts of the city by themselves—ghettos—then later shipped off to concentration camps.

That's how it had begun: first the registrations, then the round-up and finally the train rides inside box cars to concentration camps for the Final Solution. Could it happen here?

It was in that fearful mood I made my way down to the headquarters of the Los Angeles Police Department to report for registration. I was certain that, at the very least, I would probably be facing a bunch of redneck cops gulping coffee out of paper cups as they taunted me for being convicted as a child molester.

But, once in the lobby, I was politely informed by a smiling female officer at the information desk that the registration section was right down the end of the hall to my right. When I arrived there, instead of Nazi police with spike boots, I found only a mild-mannered young man who was a civilian employee. "Good morning," he said politely, as I entered. "Are you here to register?"

When I replied that I was, he invited me to step over to a desk so that he could fill out a form for me. Moments later, he took my picture and helped me leave my fingerprints on a card, gave me some special jelly and paper towels to clean my hands before leaving and wished me good luck as I left.

It'll probably get worse later, I thought, as I left the building. *They're just softening us up.*

Later events would prove I might have been right.

The Horoscope of a Sex Offender

I did individual therapy for a year, as ordered by my parole agent. I also enrolled in an adult gym to get back in shape as I'd gained too much weight while in prison. I enrolled in a business school to learn a new occupation that I could practice abroad, after parole ended, for I felt certain that I could never have a future here with a past like mine.

I studied the hospitality industry and learned hotel and restaurant management, so I could find work overseas in the tourism industry. My schedule became one of classes, gym, homework, Buddhist studies, a weekly visit to the therapist and continued studies on my own to learn more about why I'd become what I'd become as I still hadn't found all the answers I sought.

I turned to Greek tragedy and read the classic drama on incest: Sophocles' play, "Oedipus Rex," about a man doomed at birth by a prophecy that he would grow up to kill his own father and marry his mother. In spite of every step he took to outwit that fate, it came to him anyhow and destroyed his life. The message the playwright gave us was that, whatever the gods foreordain, no man can avoid. I wondered if that applied to me, so I sent for my astrological horoscope for the first time in my life.

I was shocked by what it revealed, for it showed that the reasons for my entire sexual history had been written in the stars at the very moment of my birth! The Moon in Scorpio gave me a *compulsive sexuality,* Mars in Scorpio led me to *danger and scandal,* Venus in conjunction with Uranus brought me *unconventional sexual relations with many partners,* Pluto opposite Jupiter gave me *a predatory personality* and Venus in Taurus suggested that I would become *estranged from children.*

I'd been doomed from the very start! What kind of cruel god gave a man a fate like this?

The Ancient Greeks asked that same question and, in Homer's *Iliad,* found their answer. In the character of Achilles they had a man who had been given a choice by the gods: between living a long, but anonymous life after which he would be forgotten, or a short but glorious one after which his fame would endure forever.

He chose the latter and, upon returning to battle, brought down Troy's mightiest warrior. By so doing, Achilles made possible the conquest of that kingdom. Shortly afterwards he was struck down and killed. However, his name continues to live on even today.

Homer's message was clear: we have a choice—within limits that are given to us. Astrology said the same thing when the rest of its findings were included. The sun in Gemini attracts me to *higher thoughts*, my Moon in Scorpio also leads me to *work benefiting mankind*, Mars also gives me a strong inner core of *self-reliance*, Uranus in Taurus promises me *freedom through steady growth*, Neptune in Virgo encourages me to *explore the depths* and Neptune combined with Uranus offers me *the gift of bringing forth a new vision of unity*, while Pluto in Cancer suggests a life of *marked transformation that could wipe my past clean*.

I'm given challenges, yes, but also opportunities to overcome them. Like Achilles, we are not *doomed* to our fate, but free to determine its outcome by *choosing* among the influences that come to us which ones *we* will let rule.

The Martial Art of Sexual Self-Control

To keep my sexual urges under control, I never left my premises while they were still gathering strength. Years earlier, I'd been taught some erotic exercises—readily found in many books now—that produce just as much physical satisfaction as a sex act with another person. Anyone can use them and be free afterwards to go back into the world without being ruled by sexual urges.

That was certainly better than where I'd been, years before, when I had tried to suppress all of my urges until they finally exploded. Fantasies may even be the escape valve for urges that would, otherwise, tear society apart. The trick lies in feeding them responsibly, like a pet tiger. If you try to simply starve him, he will ultimately become so desperate that he bursts his cage and devours you.

Not all sex offender therapists would agree, seeing how great a role fantasies play in the lives of some abusers, where fantasies always becomes plans to be carried out.

To keep that from happening, I always added another ingredient. After each such exercise and fantasy session, I always took a few moments to ask myself: what *really* would have happened, had I actually carried out that fantasy?

A number of answers always came to my mind: the boy in my fantasy would have told someone else, sooner or later, and I'd have gotten caught. Or, others in the neighborhood would have started noticing that I was bringing kids home, and my parole agent would come out here and take me back to prison. Or, the whole Buddhist facility would become extremely uncomfortable with my living here and simply expel me.

It would ruin my life again.

In that moment I could go back into the world, knowing that it had only been a fantasy that I would never carry out. I was self-governing now: solidly grounded back in reality, in a world where acts have consequences, and I accepted that fact.

Psychologists call such a process *aversive conditioning*—coupling an undesirable consequence to any particular act you are contemplating. The result is that you stay away from ever committing that kind of act. It works, as I soon found out when my self-control was tested the first time.

I didn't just pay rent in the form of money to the Buddhist facility. Like other residents, I also performed some of the chores required to maintain the place. Mine included taking care of the organization's two watchdogs that lived out in the back yard. I fed and watered them each day and made sure that their doghouse was heavily carpeted and well-secured against winter weather.

When neighboring schoolboys came home each day, I soon noticed that they often stopped by the back fence to say hello to the dogs and, as a result, the boys and I came to know each other, at least by sight.

One day, after having a discussion with one of the downstairs residents in my building, I went up to my room to change out of my work clothes. A moment later, there was a knock on my door. Thinking it was my fellow resident who had come up to continue our conversation I called for him to come in, even though I hadn't put my other pants completely on yet.

It was one of the boys, a 12-year old, and he had a mischievous look in his eye.

"Hi!" he chirped, as he stepped inside and glanced over at my bed. "Why don't we have a pillow fight?"

A *pillow fight*?

If my parole agent had walked in at that moment, he would have 'cuffed me and taken me right back to state prison! The rule was clear: I was not permitted to be alone with any child under fourteen years of age!

Panic began to mount but, at the same time, a wiser voice within urged me not to frighten the child. *It isn't his fault.*

It was time to use a *coping strategy*.

Quickly stepping into my pants, I replied, "That's a *great* idea, but I'll tell you what: the dogs haven't been fed yet. If you'll go downstairs and wait for me in the back yard, I'll be right down and *you* can help me feed them!"

He loved the idea, and skipped right on out…

…as I wiped the sweat off my forehead.

Afterwards, I walked him up the street to his home, where I asked him to introduce me to his family. When I met his oldest brother, I took the man outside and had a brief talk with him. I said that I thought his younger brother was a very nice little boy, but perhaps needed his brother's help right then.

I told him how the child had shown up in my room, uninvited. "These are times," I said to the older brother, gently, "when it's probably *not* best for a boy of his age to come up to the room of a man of my age, alone. It could spoil the boy's *good reputation*."

He immediately understood, and promised that he would take care of it.

"Don't scold the boy," I begged. "He did nothing wrong. He just didn't know."

The brother promised to be gentle and I thanked him and left. The problem never occurred again.

But afterwards—in a moment of singular honesty—I couldn't help but wonder if I would remain that honest, once free of the always-possible gaze of my parole agent. Would I really stay as self-controlled, when I was on my own again? Was I really in what the addiction people called *recovery* yet?

I couldn't know for sure, and for that reason, among others, when the time came to choose which country I would go to in order to find a new life when my parole was drawing to its close, I chose one where I believed the consequences wouldn't be as severe as they are here, were I to fail to stay self-controlled there.

I chose Brazil.

Was I just setting myself up for a relapse? By selecting a country where I didn't think that I'd get into that much trouble if I went back to having sex with teenage boys, was I merely *tempting* myself into doing so?

A part of myself really liked the idea of Rio de Janeiro, where there were so many *street children*.

I decided to get some advice. On the morning that I was to leave for the airport, I asked the *I Ching* what it thought about what I was going to do. In response, I received a stinging rebuke:

Have you never considered 'limitations'?

That afternoon, when I boarded the airplane to Brazil, I suddenly discovered that I had left my carry-on bag behind, on the bench in the waiting area. It held the only copy I'd packed of the *I Ching*.

"Will all passengers please take their seats?"

I had to sit down or I'd lose my flight! Even if I dashed out, there was no guarantee the bag would still be there.

"Sir?" said the stewardess, from right behind me. "Would you please go to your seat?"

The oracle of the *I Ching* was no longer speaking to me!

And Pharaoh came after the Hebrews to carry them back to Egypt.
Exodus 14:4-9.

Meeting my Adversary

Many hours later, the plane landed in Manaus, a Brazilian city in the midst of the Amazon region. My first attempt at making a new start would begin here. As I picked up my bags, I saw a young Brazilian woman approaching me, wearing the large plastic badge of a tourist guide, and I immediately put up my mental guard. All of my guidebooks had warned me not to sign up for any jungle excursions from such people because cheaper ones could be found in town. As a result, I let her know I wasn't interested the moment she began to speak.

"Besides," I told her, my mind still on that carry-on luggage I'd lost, "the first thing I have to do right now is buy some more anti-malaria medication." For that, too, had been in the bag.

"Oh!" she eagerly volunteered. "I can help you! There are only two *farmacias* in town that sell it, and I know where one is. I can drive you there!"

It seemed strange to me that, in the middle of the Amazon Jungle, there'd only be two places where anti-malarial medication would be sold, but I decided I'd better take her offer, as I didn't know where either of them were located.

"Okay," I said. "But I don't want to buy any excursions."

She nodded understandingly and escorted me toward the doors of the terminal. The moment we stepped outside, the jungle's scorching air hit me like a blast furnace.

"*Quente!*" I said, the Portuguese word for "hot."

"*Sim,*" she replied, the Portuguese word for "yes." I'd spent my last six months on parole taking an audio course in that language and it was a pleasure to begin using it.

It didn't take long for us to reach downtown Manaus, a modern-looking metropolis hacked right out of the jungle that waits patiently behind it—like a crouching cheetah—to pounce on it and take it back at any time.

True to her word, my companion delivered me to a pharmacy where they sold what I was looking for. But, afterwards, she asked if I would walk "just a couple of doors down the street" to meet her boss, "so he won't feel I wasted my time today."

How convenient that his office was so close! But I owed her for her help, and the ride into the city, so I went with her just to meet the man. I certainly wasn't going to sign up for any excursions without checking around first and I would say so, if asked.

His name was Armando and from his first words I could tell that he was in love with the Amazon Jungle. Lean, tall, dark-haired, he instantly held me spellbound as he told of all the wonders that the jungle offered. I was so impressed by his delivery that I signed up for an excursion that would leave in just three days.

In return, he had the young woman get on the phone and book me a hotel room that wound up costing me only half of what I'd been prepared to pay. They even gave me a ride over there.

It was a fine little place, only a fifteen-minute walk from the Amazon River. Anxious to see that magnificence, I quickly unpacked my luggage and made my way down to its shores.

The mighty Amazon River is a breathtaking sight as it flows on past. The city's largest marketplace sits high above its banks here. Underneath a long, shady roof, row after row of every kind of meat, fish, vegetable and fruit grown or caught anywhere in the region sits on display. Everything in the Amazon is either brought here or carried away by riverboat. It has to be sold fast, though, as the heat and humidity doesn't let anything keep for very long.

The river is the jungle's artery, feeding it from Peru in the west to the Atlantic Ocean in the east, 2500 miles away from its beginning. Every evening at sunset, people go down to the river and drink a toast to her, using a local beer kept just above freezing. It's called *cerveza gelado*, which means 'frozen beer,' and in between its rich cold temperature and high alcoholic boost, it's like an ice pack made to smother the heat inside you.

"*Ele vai a Peru,*" the people sing out, as they raise their bottles in salute to the setting sun. "*He goes to Peru!*"

I bought a beer right then, in the middle of the day, and sat on top of a low wall to enjoy the view. The heat had drenched the back of my thin cotton shirt and the beer flowed sweetly into me as I sat there and looked at the scene before me: the boats, the men, the River…the Power of my life!

An old man glanced at me as he walked past and I politely raised my beer in salute. In response, he taught me my first Amazon wisdom: "If you keep looking at the river long enough," he said, "you will see all your old enemies go floating on by!"

Several days later, I went into the jungle on my excursion through one of the river's fingers that poked at the city's edge. Armando had guides take us in by canoe and the moment we reached our lodge I asked him if I could leave it to step into the bush.

He smiled knowingly, for he understood the spell that called. "Just don't go too far," he said. "And, if you see any animals, don't forget that this is not a zoo! Here, they will eat you."

I promised to take care and hiked on over to our compound's border. Gently pushing my way through some of the waiting shrubbery, I stepped into the jungle and found myself in an entirely pristine and primitive world: of plants and vines and jousting treetops whose branches all pushed and shoved at each other in their struggle to get to the life-giving sunlight high above.

Not far ahead, I saw a tree at least sixty or seventy feet tall and went over to sit underneath it, just to let myself meditate in the jungle's steamy cleanliness. A small rivulet of the Amazon flowed silently past. The stillness about me was so great that I could almost touch it.

At first. But then, high above in the canopy, I suddenly heard the crackling noises of dry leaves being rudely kicked off as a small troop of tree monkeys scampered on across. Tan, dusty leaves swirled lazily down in their wake, falling to the ground nearby, where waiting platoons of army ants quickly chopped them up and marched them back to their nest. In the jungle, everything comes back to the soil, which is both grave and womb of life.

A vision appeared in my mind, of a giant sitting in front of me, insanely devouring his own foot while a new one grew out from behind him.

I took heart from the message I saw in this: that life is self-renewing only through being self-destroying. It *can't* recreate itself without first destroying itself; like a snake that sheds its skin so that a new one can come forth. Self-destruction leads to self-renewal. Our lives are *built* to fail—repeatedly—so that they may succeed over and over again. I still had a chance!

I spent almost a week there, hiking through the bush and gazing with wonder at huge rubber trees and brightly-colored parrots. I was taken to a small waterfall where I let myself have a natural shower underneath it. Afterwards, while making my way along the trail back to camp, I came across a gigantic spider web almost two yards wide. All along its many strands I could see dozens of tiny insects stuck to it, quivering for their lives. I paused to watch as Mother Death came creeping down to have her late afternoon meal.

Armando saw my look of pity and said, "Do not waste your sympathies on them. They are *Anopheles.*"

The mosquitoes that carry malaria?

"*Bon appetit!*" I called to the spider, and walked past her uncaringly. May she eat all of them.

A few days later, I was back in the city, only to find that I had now contracted Jungle Fever. I woke up with it in my hotel room at dawn, hot and very ill. I found my thermometer and could barely believe what it told me: I had a temperature of 102 degrees Fahrenheit. Quickly, I took two aspirins and lay down, falling asleep for a couple of hours. When I woke up, I took my temperature again.

It was 105.

It should be *down!*

The aspirins weren't having any effect and I knew that I was in danger. If I didn't get some medication right away, brain damage would occur and then death.

Forcing myself to get dressed, I stumbled out of the hotel into a waiting taxi, and had it take me down to Armando's, as he was the only person I knew.

The moment I appeared in his doorway, he got up from his desk.

"You look terrible!" he said.

I told him what was happening and he came over, felt my forehead and gestured toward the door. "We'll go to the *farmacia.*"

He bought me something from West Germany: forty drops poured into a glass of juice and my fever immediately began to cascade down. By the next morning it was normal. Armando came by and urged me to convalesce. "You're still getting used to our climate and its biological system," he said. "It's totally different than the one in which you live in North America, with many germs your body hasn't experienced before. Rest some more"

I thanked him, then asked a question I had been wondering about since first arriving here. "How come there are only two *farmacias* that sell antimalaria medication?"

He laughed gently to himself before replying, "Because they don't need it here. They conquered malaria in this city many years ago. Only *tourists* buy it now."

I did as he said and took it easy for the next week or so, staying close to my hotel. When the day came that I felt well enough to do so, I went back on down to the Amazon River, thinking I might have a cold beer there and perhaps something simple to eat.

The moment I stepped through the ornate gate to its market place, however, I was besieged by a whole swarm of local shoeshine boys, ten or eleven years old, all of whom began petitioning for my business at once. In response, I brushed them away like mosquitoes. But then, from out of the shadows, another boy stepped forward, smiling wickedly. He looked to be about fourteen or fifteen years old and moved his slim little hips like a Latin dance as he approached.

Immediately, I was frozen to the spot.

All over the world there are boys like him, wise beyond their years in the ways of the street. Sexually used since who-knows-when, they know that an older man, traveling alone, is a likely customer and they move like a spider in the jungle toward their own *Anopheles*.

The gleam in his eyes transfixed me and I could feel my self-control losing its solidity and getting ready to melt away. Within seconds, I would just be an urge again.

Suddenly, my bright new life flashed in front of me—the adventures I was having in the jungle, my new friendship with Armando, the welcoming staff at my hotel, a deferential police officer, up at the plaza, who always tipped his cap to me as I strolled past each morning—all this would vanish if I lost control.

The boy would boast to his friends, who would tell their older brothers, who would beat and rob me while police looked the other way, if they didn't shake me down for money themselves. Instead of being a welcome guest, I would become everyone's prey.

I was at that *threshold magnitude* of which Solzhenytsin had written. Had I gone so far past it that I couldn't make my way back now?

The boy continued to dance toward me and I knew there were only seconds left before I compulsively went off with him.

Looking deeply within myself for some way, any way, out—I plunged my right hand into my pants pocket and pulled out a fist-full of coins that I hurled over his head. He immediately turned to look as all the other boys hungrily followed their arc through the air, and then rushed to join them as everyone chased after them...leaving me free to turn around and walk quietly back to my hotel, still whole.

I was no longer just an urge. I had finally attained *personhood* and was self-governing now.

Encoded within everyone's life is the life of Another. Finding that 'other' and learning to dance with it may be the purpose of living. But so is knowing when to sit this one out.

*   *   *

How to Protect Your Children

1. Teach your children never to go into any neighbor's home alone unless they have playmates there and their parents or care-provider are known to you as trustworthy.
2. Teach your children that they have choices as to what happens to them and that they can ask you for help in making them.
3. Ask your children where they have been each day after school so you know where they are going and who they are seeing.
4. Make it your business to know the adults your children have contact with, even if they are other parents. It is imperative that you know what kinds of homes your children are visiting.
5. Don't go on vacation as a parent when you take your children with you on vacation, especially in a foreign country.
6. Don't allow your children to go off with any hotel or cruise ship employee unless there are at least two of them supervising the children, preferably of the opposite sex, or go with them.

*　　　　　*　　　　　*

Questions to Consider

1. What can families do to help one of its relatives convicted of a sex offense complete parole successfully?
2. What can neighbors do?
3. What could you do, if such a person was living next to you?
4. What can we ask of neighborhood churches, houses of worship, civics groups, women's groups, or service organizations?

Chapter Eight

The Polite Interrogation

It wasn't long until my growing friendship with Armando brought me a job working for his tourist agency, just as I'd hoped. Every time tourists were signed up, I was one of the guides who went out with them into the same jungle I'd first visited.

It was good work and I enjoyed it immensely. It was fascinating to see how different tourists were who came from other countries. The easiest ones to work with were the Germans. They were very adaptive people, friendly, and had a rich sense of humor.

One time, we had a German statistician with us on one of our outings. Promptly at 6:00 p.m. every night, no matter where we were, he took out his short wave receiver and tuned in to Radio Hamburg for no more than a couple of minutes. Since we were in the middle of the Amazon Jungle, I asked him why he bothered.

He replied in all seriousness, "To get the value of the day's Deutschmark!"

I couldn't imagine why. A few days later, we came upon a jungle hut in which a native family lived. They gave us permission to come in and see it in exchange for a few coins. Our statistician became excited when he saw that they also had a small short wave receiver on an upper shelf in their kitchen.

"Ask them vhat they listen to!" he urged me.

When they replied, in Brazilian Portuguese—which he couldn't understand—he begged me to translate it for him. "Vhat did they say?"

"They said," I told him, in all seriousness, "that they listen to Radio Hamburg, to get the value of the day's Deutschmark."

"Nein!" my friend insisted, laughing as hard as he could. "You lie! I can tell."

The most difficult tourists were the Americans. They were afraid to touch anything if they weren't sure it was absolutely clean. Which, in the middle of the Amazon Jungle, is a bit of a problem. No one fusses more than they do.

One small group from the States insisted they had to have "authentic Brazilians" as their guides, on a day when all of the other men were already out with other customers. Armando was beside himself. "What shall I do?"

Affecting my best Brazilian-Portuguese, I said, "*Todo bem* (all is well). I can take them."

He smiled mischievously. "Do you think it will work?"

"They don't speak Brazilian Portuguese! And, when I speak to them in English, I'll just fake my accent."

Ten minutes later, the Americans were traveling with me in the agency car. It was only a day trip, but they enjoyed it and, at the end, even gave me a tip of ten U.S. dollars. When the other guides heard the story, they loved it!

It was the only money I'd see, though. Often short of jobs themselves, foreign countries rarely let foreigners come there to work, except under very special conditions, such as when the foreigner has a very rare skill or is already employed by the same company in the United States and is only being transferred to its overseas branch here.

Since I fell in neither of those categories, the law prevented any employer from paying me in cash. What they could do was pay 'in kind,' such as by giving the foreigner free rent, if the employer owns a hotel, or free meals, if he has a restaurant. Here, the only 'hotel' was out in the jungle, not in the city, and was impossible to stay at full-time, so it wasn't a job that would really support me.

My attempt at making it into one soon came to the attention of authorities, however, and it wasn't long before I had a visit from a police inspector at my hotel.

He was very polite and invited me to have a beer with him up the street, where we sat down. There, he showed me his badge, which was about as large as a dinner plate.

"Inspector Cambalacho," he said, introducing himself.

He asked how long I'd been in the country, asked me to show him my passport and visa, which I was glad to do. Then he said, "I notice your visa only gives you tourist privileges, not employment rights."

I nodded in agreement, as he handed my papers back to me.

"May you continue to enjoy our country," he said, raising his beer to me in a toast, "*as a tourist.*"

I got the message, and began spending less time at Armando's and more with myself.

I found a book in Portuguese and began translating a part of it each day, to improve my language skills. At night, I took a break from my studies by wandering up the street to the nearby cantina where I could sit at one of its outdoor tables.

Rarely was I left alone very long. In addition to the some of the locals who were naturally curious about people from other countries, the streets were flooded each night with hordes of little boys, ages ten and under, all with trays hung around their necks, upon which sat tiny packets of chewing gum or small bags of peanuts to sell which they had shelled and rolled themselves. While all of these children needed charity, none of them sought it. Poor, they certainly deserved it. But the Brazilians are a proud people and do not ask for anything without offering something in return.

Since there were so many of these little boys, I knew it would be impossible to buy from all of them, so I did as the locals did. Every time I saw a child approaching my table, I waved the forefinger of my left hand back and forth in the air a couple of times, in a gesture which they knew meant: do not disturb me now. It always worked.

That is, until one night when one little boy walked up to me and refused to go away.

Curious, I finally looked up and what I saw was the pain in his eyes. He was ten years old, with blond hair and brown eyes, and right then it was obvious that, if he didn't get a victory, his little soul would shatter.

I nodded with a knowing smile and took some coins from my pocket as I recalled how all the guidebooks had urged me to always be generous here. You pay more for your airline ticket, they cautioned, than most of these people earn in a year. As a result, they think you are a millionaire and expect you to share some of what you have. It is only good manners to do so.

That's when I decided to buy from this child, regularly, as my representative of all the rest. I told him that he could sell to me from now on, whenever he saw me.

He smiled gratefully and went away. But, as he did so, I confessed to myself that I also found him potentially attractive. *In just a few years…*

That's what it's like to be a sex offender in recovery. That's what it means, when you are told that our condition can be *managed*, but not cured. It will continually sneak back up on us, if we aren't extremely watchful. Remaining aware of that is what lets us stay in charge of it.

I saw the boy next a few evenings later on an especially hot night with a humidity that was smothering. Because of the unusual heat, I asked him if he would like a cold soda drink and he smiled his assent. I signaled to a passing waiter to give him a soft drink, on my bill and the boy thanked me sincerely. But when the bottle arrived and he was about to raise it, he suddenly halted.

Spying two little cousins across the street, he signaled for them to come over and then, in spite of the fact that it was a scorching night and this was his only drink, he let each of them take a drink first.

His unselfishness was so great that it shamed me into finding my own and I immediately stopped entertaining any further thought of using him as a sexual target. I respected him, instead, subsequently learning that he had several brothers and sisters with whom he lived, along with his mother. I never heard anything about his father and knew better than to ask.

In the mornings he went to school, in the afternoons he shined shoes, and in the evenings carried a tray around his neck and sold gum or small sacks of peanuts to contribute what he could to his family's income.

He said that he wanted to become an airline pilot when he grew up and fly huge airplanes that crossed whole continents. I told him that, if he wanted to enough, *he could even have the stars!*

My recovery was solidifying and I never got to Rio de Janeiro to go after any of its street children.

It wasn't much later that I learned the Portuguese word for the intimate form of the pronoun "you"—used between lovers—is the very same word I had used years before to name my sexual compulsion: *voce.* (Pronounced the same way, vo-SAY.) Yet I'd never spoken or known Portuguese before this time.

How could I have used it so accurately years ago unless something in me—something in all of us that knows all languages—spoke it to me?

Apparently, consciousness was trying to tell me the same thing it had whispered to the Sufi poet, Rumi, eight centuries before—that our creator and we do not finally meet somewhere, but are in each other all along.

What's necessary is that we accept the fact that it has a dark side, too.

The Polite Interrogation

When my visa expired, I went north to Costa Rica and that's when I first began writing this book. While on parole I had made one new friend in Los Angeles and told him that I'd just gotten out of prison, but not why. He was decent enough not to ask. But he did say that if I ever chose to write my story I could send it to him; if it was commercial enough he would send it to an agent he knew and have it published. Having no other options, I decided to start writing it.

I rented a room in a house, just outside the capital city, bought a used electric typewriter and began the book there. The landlady was an executive secretary, employed in town and away every day, or seeing her relatives on weekends, so I had all the peace and quiet I needed to do my work. Kitchen privileges came with the rent and a small grocery store down the street supplied me with everything I needed. On Fridays, I took the day off and went into town to do banking and any errands that were necessary.

I always included a nice meal at the end of that day. One time, reading an English-language newspaper over coffee, I spotted a notice announcing weekly worship services for Americans overseas at a local Jewish temple. Homesick by now, I went over there and enjoyed the experience so much that I began returning regularly. But in the social hour afterwards, I found myself so on guard against saying anything about my past that I was unable to make any but the most distant of new acquaintances.

Only in the movies does one effortlessly slip away to a foreign country and begin a new life. In the real world, one's past sticks to them. When it's not a nice past there are always the awkward questions, the social inquiries one faces whenever one meets new people abroad.

"What did you do in the States?"

"Are you married?"

"Do you have any children?"

Additional questions always follow until the other person has sorted and filed you into a known category. *Oh, a retired businessman. I see. A lawyer? How nice.*

What was I going to tell them? That I was a *Retired sex offender?*

Of course, in answering, one could always lie about one's past (and anyone escaping their past always wants to do that). But if you do, you'll quickly realize that the burden of having to remember all the lies you told soon becomes too great for anyone without a laptop computer. ("Oh—I said that I have *three* children? Well, actually that's true, but my second wife also had two of her own from an earlier marriage and *that's* why I often say that I have five…worked there instead of here…lived in that city instead of this one…")

One who really wishes to be rid of one's past doesn't actually get rid of it; one learns instead how to 'minimize' it by saying no more than is absolutely essential to social discourse and then changing the subject.

That works, and as a result one passes the moment of inquisition. But, afterwards, there is always that sense of *distance* still out there which leaves you as uncomfortable as it does relieved that you didn't have to discuss what you wished would just go away. And because it's always possible that someone from your past might just show up—on *their* vacation—you always keep your suitcase open in case you have to pack hurriedly.

Of course, you can always avoid your fellow countrymen and just socialize with locals, if you know the language (or they know yours, which is more often the case). That works, as the language barrier exempts you from having to go into the details of your past. No one expects you to know the local language so well that you could refer to all the details of anything, including your past. Thus, one can always use the foreign language to say "I don't understand your question" when asked something one would really prefer not to have to answer, and get away with it.

But you still know who you are; you don't forget that, or the life you've lived up until then. You're reminded of it all the time, wherever you go. You're on a bus going into town and see a woman walking along the pavement with two little boys, one holding onto each of her hands. Instantly, you flash back to your own wife of years ago, and your sons when they were with her and—what do you know?—emotionally, you're right back home again, in your own country and not anywhere near the Third World refuge you thought you'd found.

Key holidays such as Christmas and New Year's are celebrated everywhere and destroy any possibility of forgetting one's past. So, no, that quaint romantic notion that one can easily fly into a foreign country and effortlessly become someone else is just the cheap fiction of paperback novels and movies based only on fantasies. One never leaves their past, for it is as much a part of them as their skin. All one can do is wear a coat over it and squirm inside every time you meet anyone from your own country and they begin to pursue that polite interrogation.

When my visa in Costa Rica expired, I moved to Mexico to finish writing the manuscript. Just before I left Costa Rica, I sent a letter to my friend in L.A. and told him all about the rest of my past.

When the time later came that I felt the manuscript was ready to be seen, I flew up to L.A. and hand-delivered it to him.

He refused to accept it because of what he had learned from my letter. "I could have forgiven you for what you were sent to prison for," he said, hurt and angry. "But not for your having kept it from me for so long, as if you didn't trust me. Our friendship is at an end. I don't ever want to see you again."

I left his company, feeling crushed, even though it was my fault and I knew it. Totally without hope, I dumped the manuscript in a trashcan in back of a supermarket in Hollywood, and went on my way. Still shunned by my family, I stayed at a hotel. By the time a week had passed I was so despondent that I began to consider going back to living as a sexual predator again since nothing else seemed to offer any reason not to do so. The same old process had kicked in once more: like any other sex offender, whenever I became too depressed, lust arose as its antidote. You might want to consider that, the next time someone suggests that the best way to handle registered sex offenders is simply by driving them away.

I went to a bookstore and bought myself some travel books to find a destination. In reading about various places in Central America, I came across an orphanage that allowed anyone to live there while serving as a volunteer.

Kids! Living with them.

My mind caught on fire at the very thought of it.

Yes. That's where I'll go. The hell with this! Being a sex offender is all I've got. That's who I really am.

The Third World is full of European and American child molesters, working in settlement projects, orphanages and any other place where they can nurse their sexual addiction until they die, or go mad, or get killed. I felt ready to become one of them and take my place in the armies of the lonely.

I made my way down to Mexico City that week, in the first leg of my new journey. But the further I got from the toxic atmosphere of rejection I'd just left behind, the less the whole purpose of the trip appealed to me. By the time I reached Mexico City, I was absolutely repulsed by the notion. Freed from everything that had depressed me, my wholeness had returned.

But where was I to go now?

A local Jewish family provided the answer. They invited me to join them for a Sabbath dinner in their home and, when I got there, I found myself surrounded by all their many relatives, a number of whom had been to Israel several times. When the oldest uncle present leaned over his soup bowl to ask me if I had ever gone there, all I could say was, "Not yet."

He looked back at me, leaving a tablespoon suspended in mid-air. "What are you waiting for? *That's the only place where a Jew can find a new life!*"

I flew there the very next day, certain that this time my past would not come with me.

A lot of people have troubled pasts in Israel that they don't want to talk about, I thought to myself. People will understand.

Sure, if you've come from The Holocaust. But today?

Ambushed By My Past

Upon arrival at the Tel Aviv-Jerusalem Airport, a hand gently clasped my shoulder as I spoke to the operator on a pay phone to let my family's attorney know I was here now.

I turned my head to see who was touching me and beheld a young man with a crew cut who spoke with an accent. "Israeli Security," he said. "You've got to leave the airport."

'*Because I'm a convicted sex offender?*' I thought to myself, in alarm. '*They know?*'

As I looked around, I saw others like him hustling hordes of fellow tourists outside.

No! I suddenly realized. *It's because there's a bomb threat!*

I quickly turned and followed the crowd out into the street.

A fellow tourist in her early forties stood in the roadway outside of the airport, clutching her baggage cart. She was frozen into place by terror and I comforted her. "There's nothing to fear," I told her as I approached. "We're safe." I could feel it.

She blinked and came back to where we were. "What should we do?"

I looked up the street and said, "Why don't we join the others?"

She pushed her baggage cart ahead of her as the two of us walked up there. Thanks to what she later told me over a cup of coffee when the emergency was past, I learned of a great place to stay in nearby Jerusalem and hailed a cab to make my way over there.

It's a fabulous city of more than 600,000 people. Actually, it's two cities: one inside the other. There's the modern metropolis and, at its core, the walled Old City, hearkening back to Biblical times. The older one was the one into which I was heading. When my taxi stopped and I looked out its window, I found myself staring at stone walls with slits cut in them, through which arrows could be fired! On top, the wall was punctuated with gaps where men could stand to pour boiling oil down onto any who tried to climb up ladders and invade it. The city still had wooden gates to it and the one I saw was huge: inside a tall almond-shaped arch sealed off but for a narrow opening at its bottom through which you had to walk as no car could drive there.

"This is where you get out," my taxi driver told me. "I can't drive any closer."

I grabbed my bags and paid him, then walked towards it. Crowds of Arabs were streaming in and out and, once inside its courtyard, I saw carts full of merchandise all about me, with their vendors noisily hawking their goods as people haggled loudly with them.

It was like suddenly being in another era!

My hotel was on a street called *El Wad Road* and I had to find it.

"Excuse me," I begged a nearby merchant at his stand. "Can you tell me where 'El Wad Road' is?"

He glared back at me impatiently. "You're standing on it!"

Three blocks down, I found my hotel.

I happily booked a room for myself with a view of the entire city from the building's rooftop. Once unpacked, I headed back out into the tiny cramped streets no bigger than alleyways to tramp my way into ancient history with each step, for many of the stones upon which I walked had been placed there by any number of conquerors who had walked here before: Egyptians, Romans, Turks, Crusaders, Germans and later the British.

Even Christ had walked here.

I bought a ticket and climbed on top of the city's walls and walked around the whole place, seeing two kinds of history at the same time, the ancient city inside and the modern city, outside.

I visited the Church of the Holy Sepulcher, where Christ was said to have been crucified. I meandered through a humble Ethiopian monastery. And I edged my way through a long stone tunnel that finally emerged into an open courtyard as large as several city blocks, where the Western Wall of King Solomon's Temple stands majestically in the distance. Every Friday night, the city's most religious Jews pray there.

I was charmed by Jerusalem but it was an expensive charm. In spite of its Third World location, its prices were more like those of Beverly Hills and I soon found that my funds would not sustain me unless I lived in more modest quarters. A move to a much simpler place, where the owner gave me a discount on my room in exchange for manning the front desk at night, provided the remedy.

Up on the top floor, there was a dormitory with a lot of college-age kids from Europe and the United States who were backpacking their way around the Middle East in the last years before the present war. They were the ones who made me earn my pay. At night, especially on the weekends, they naturally wanted to leave the Old City and go into the newer one, to dance at its various discos and meet Israeli kids. Since our guests were from the First World, when they went out they saw no reason not to dress the same way they did at home, with girls wearing particularly revealing clothing.

This caused a problem, for in the Old City the Arabs were not First World, or the least bit modern, particularly the Arab women who still wore burkas and kept their faces hidden. When they saw how daringly—in their eyes—our girls dressed, they were shocked and told their sons that these girls were no better than prostitutes.

Believing them, the young Arab boys began to chase after the girls and taunt them as they came back from the discos late at night, stroking them, pinching them, frightening them.

I tried to explain to the girls that, since they were in the Arabs' part of the city, it might be better if they wore a long coat over themselves whenever they went out, and some did. Some didn't, insisting that they had the right to wear anything they pleased, and there were some ugly incidents.

One of our girls came home late one night, in tears and with the top of her dress ripped. She had almost been raped. I went to the Israeli police the next day and got them to post two guards at the city gate our girls used and the problem ended.

The girls appreciated that and, from then on, a number of them came down late at night—in one's and two's—just to talk with me. They'd speak of their hopes, their dreams, their past, the kinds of things that kids of that age will often talk about.

I was glad to listen, for it took my mind off my off own life. I never had to talk about it now in any detail as their conversations let me rest in an anonymity I truly welcomed.

On my next Friday night off I made my way back to the Wall of King Solomon's Temple. When I got there, I left my late father's name written down on a slip of paper that I rolled up and inserted between two large stones in the wall, as is the custom. After I did so, I pressed the side of my face against the wall and closed my eyes, just to commune with it, I guess. I really don't know why I did it, but it seemed like the right thing to do at that moment.

The stones were refreshingly cool, and as smooth as eternity. All around me, others prayed in Hebrew.

A moment passed, then two. And, out of the very center of my consciousness, I suddenly heard my own voice inside my head, speaking to me as if I were a stranger. In a very loud whisper, all by itself it proclaimed: *"I AM!"*

Startled, I stepped back from the Wall and acknowledged the power it held with a respectful nod of my head. Then I turned around and began to walk back through the dark Mediterranean night to my hotel.

"I Am," I thought to myself, as I made my way along the ancient stone passageway. "I Am…what?" That's what I needed to know, for I was lost in my life, without any direction, and I knew it very sadly.

The answer was waiting for me when I got back. That night, one of our guests—a college co-ed from London—came down to talk with me and spoke of her memories. At first they were gentle ones and then—all of a sudden—her eyes began to mist and her voice cracked.

"Oh, Jake!" she sobbed out. "How am I ever going to love my father again? He *molested* me when I was only five years old!"

I was struck dumb by her question. It was as if my past was suddenly standing there, pointing its long accusatory finger directly at me. My run was over and I knew it. No matter where I went, it would always be waiting to ambush me again. There would always be another moment like this, when it would unexpectedly appear, there would always be some other person to ask me that same kind of question. It was time to face that fact and accept my past instead of trying to hide it.

The message that came to me from the Wall was now complete: I am my past. I can't deny that without denying myself, and I would never do so again.

I flew back to the United States the following week, determined to use my past as the foundation for the only decent life I saw that I could have now: working with other men who have similar pasts so that we might keep them from becoming anything more than our past.

*   *   *

How to Protect Your Children

1. Don't let your daughters dress so daringly, or ahead of their age, that they are bait for an ugly incident. Not everyone is First World, even in our country and some men can't handle it when they behold an attractive teen. Don't tempt them. No 12-year old should be allowed by her parents to dress as if she's 20 years old, because she hasn't got the mental faculties and experience of a 20-year old to handle what a 20-year old attracts.

   No, this is not to 'excuse' the rapist, or 'encourage' rape. Facts are facts: a child dressing like a young woman can't handle what a young woman attracts and she can wait until she is one to dress like that. It really won't kill her, but ignoring this warning might.

2. Don't drive away former sex offenders living in recovery or you risk discouraging them to the point where they will lapse and strike again.

3. Tell your legislators that you want convicted former sex offenders to have a place where they can meet and be in an ongoing recovery group in your city and county.

4. Make it possible for sex offenders to get post-parole counseling from mental health agencies.

*   *   *

Questions to Consider

1. What are some of the things that might cause a recovering sex offender to give up?
2. Do you believe that our lives are designed to succeed over their failures?
3. Can a former sex offender build a new life?
4. Could you bring yourself to tell someone else that *you* once committed a sexual offense, if that were true?

Chapter Nine

Sex Offender in the Community

It was not a good time to be a convicted sex offender. From Australia to the United Kingdom and throughout the United States, there had been a stream of ugly incidents against us. Pickets had appeared, demanding we move, realtors were afraid to sell our houses, and in England a fourteen-year-old girl died after the building in which she had been staying was burned down after having been mistakenly identified as one harboring some of us. Cries went up, demanding that we all be rounded up and expelled, either to a special town of our own or to an island from which we'd never be allowed to leave.

In the previous regime in South Africa, a similar policy banning all Black people from living in the cities was called *apartheid*. What I was looking at now was *sexual apartheid*.

How strange. Almost all of us had originally been victims of sexual abuse and, in Western society, when you're a victim of sexual abuse, people feel great sympathy for you. But the moment it turns out that the damage we received passes through us and damages someone else, we find we are no longer considered victims.

"They're like *Dracula*!" declared one judge in a case I'd worked.

If he'd meant the kind described by novelist Anne Rice, he'd have been right. The vampires in her novels don't choose to become vampires, they're made into them by someone who already is one. Similarly, among all the sex offenders I've met—in the jails, through the mail, on the Internet or in the streets—there's never been one yet who was able to tell me that he *chose* to become a sex offender. We don't *choose* our sexual inclination any more than you do.

Confirmation can be found in the work of one of America's top therapists for sex offenders, Dr. Fred Berlin, of Johns Hopkins University School of Medicine, in Baltimore, Maryland, whose sex offender treatment clinic has the lowest re-offense rate in this nation. According to his findings, no one chooses their sexual tastes:

"The author, for example, is a man who is attracted exclusively to females rather than males. Although he might find a broad age range of females to be appealing in a sexual way, he is not attracted to four-year-old females, nor is he attracted sexually to eighty-year-old females. Thus he does not refrain from having sex with young children only because he is a moral person. He is simply not tempted sexually by young children…

"If one looks at a group of children who have been active sexually with adults, thankfully most do not grow up to"…become child molesters. However, modern day sex offender therapist pioneer A.N. Groth and others have shown that "if one looks at a group of men who are child molesters…the overwhelming majority were active sexually with adults during childhood. Thus, if one wishes to use words such as victim and victimizer, it appears that many men with pedophilic sexual orientations are in fact simply the former victims of sexual abuse during childhood, grown up….sexual orientation is much like language…Once (it)…has been acquired (it)…cannot simply be made to go away."

As Dr. Berlin concludes:

"Thus it seems difficult to see how a person could be considered blameworthy because he is sexually attracted to children. However, it could be argued that although it is not his *fault* that he is sexually attracted to children, it is still his *responsibility* to resist succumbing to such temptations."

I agree wholeheartedly.

Levels of Recovery

Upon returning from Jerusalem, I landed in Los Angeles where I was tested again. On a walk by myself the next afternoon, I saw three boys in their late teens across the street. Two of them seemed to be trying to urge the third to do something, while glancing at me, repeatedly. My danger signals came on. A moment later, the third boy turned my way and began coming over to my side of the street: a blond-haired kid, about seventeen, I guessed.

He was carrying himself rather awkwardly and when he came up to me I could see that he had beads of perspiration on his upper lip, which told me he was scared.

He asked me with a bit of hesitation if he could have some money and I knew it was his first time. That I could easily take him back to my room and get away with using him was clear: no one else was around who knew me, I'd be flying out the next day and these kids would never find me. And he wasn't a bad-looking boy, certainly attractive enough to consider.

But when I looked inside of myself, I found a *firewall* present that had never been there before, and it wouldn't give way. My recovery had strengthened.

"No," I replied firmly, and the boy turned around and walked back to his friends somewhat sheepishly as they stood there, not quite knowing what to do. I could resume living safely in my country now, although I would always have to remain on guard.

Recovery doesn't happen on just one level. It goes on and becomes recovery on many levels. First, it may be no more than a fear of getting arrested again and sent back to prison. Then, it may be a matter of not wanting to lose whatever self-esteem you've been able to find. Later, it becomes a concern for those you might otherwise victimize. Ultimately, it goes on to become an awareness of how much harm you would also be causing their families as well as those who have trusted you to remain self-governing. Recovery never ends. It just keeps deepening until you don't want to do anything more than honor your new life by taking care of it.

That doesn't mean you won't be tempted at times. Like every human being, as long as your heart beats you will have urges that come to you. Most of the time they will be quickly passing ones, of no concern. Occasionally, they may be threatening and that is when your training pays off. I told Oprah that no one can say *for certain* that they won't re-offend, because sex offending isn't curable. That means there will always be a chance of relapse for any of us, no matter how small. As a result, when she found that I had given a former victim my vow never to re-offend, that troubled her as it seemed to conflict with what I'd already said.

The fault was mine: I hadn't expressed myself clearly enough. While it's true that there will always be a chance of relapse—making it impossible to say with *absolute* certainty that I won't re-offend—by giving someone my vow, what I'm telling them is that it is still my *intention* never to do so. And that's what makes it worth giving. But the question she was pursuing is an essential one: can we ever trust sex offenders again?

Marc Klaas, the father of a girl murdered by a sex offender, answered it best. Speaking on television about me later, he said that while he respected my recovery, he would never want his family to use me to take care of any of their children, and I say that is absolutely *sane*. In some tasks, it's just inviting disaster to ask someone with a known temptation to serve. In others, there's no reason not to use them.

I would never take a job as a boy's high school swim coach. That would be accepting an invitation to a likely relapse. But that doesn't mean I can't serve in other work. It doesn't mean that those convicted of sex offenses can't work in jobs where they won't be in contact with anyone likely to be hurt by them. Obviously, if they are not given any kind of work, they will join the armies of the desperate, far too large already out on our streets. One man I know of, who was convicted of being a Sexually Violent Predator and has now been released from mental hospital confinement, is currently seeking work that he can do on his computer from out of his home. That could be an excellent job for him as long as his work is honest. There is no reason for anyone else not to use him.

We cannot afford to have an underclass in our society. A divided society is not something we can afford. What keeps a society great is its ability to heal, and that means it must heal its people, even (maybe especially) those injured by mental conditions they never chose. Twenty-one hundred years ago, a great man died on a cross to teach resurrection. We crucify him again every time we deny resurrection to anyone else.

No Dishonest Friendships

My recovery began to flourish when I settled in San Francisco. I found a room in the center of town, rode the cable car into Chinatown and took a bus across the Golden Gate Bridge to go hiking in a nearby redwood forest. I began attending worship services at an ecumenical inner city church, where its legendary pastor welcomed me after I had confided in him and told him of my past.

Not certain that others would be as charitable, I decided to behave only as a guest in the community and not as one of its equals. *Toleration* was what I'd seek for now. I would let acceptance wait until later. In my relationships with others, I began living by a new rule: *no dishonest friendships.* Having already lost one good friend because I had waited too long to tell him about my past, I decided that I'd rather not have any friendships if the only kind I could have were those based on concealment. So I kept my watch and whenever I saw anyone approaching that line transforming an acquaintance into a friend, I'd tell them about my past, with an apology, and let them know that I didn't intend to repeat it.

They appreciated such a disclosure, and let me have a place among them. And as word about me got around, women who had been sexually abused began seeking me out just to listen to them respectfully, as they narrated an account of their own suffering. Afterwards, each time, I apologized to them—as if I had been their abuser—for I knew that I could have been, and they accepted that. As a result, both of us went away feeling a bit more healed.

So it happened that, when the law was changed to require not only the *registration* of sex offenders but *dissemination of their residential locations* to the public—under *Megan's Law*—it was easy for me to endorse it and I did so, speaking in the press and on television from the time it came into force.

I'd already seen how terrified parents were. I understood the depth of their fear. They had to be given something they could do to overcome it—some hands-on tool they could use to at least believe they could protect their children from being abducted, and worse.

Under our Constitution, the government has a duty to ensure *domestic tranquility. Megan's Law* was the means that government chose to do so. If it hasn't succeeded fully yet, the fault doesn't lie in that law but in some of the ways it has been applied and those can be corrected.

Yes, I'm aware that, by its disclosure of our past crimes, *Megan's Law* flies in the face of a long-standing tradition of letting a man make a new start after he's paid for his crimes. If all we were talking about here was a thief, I'd agree. But so long as sex offending is not curable, we can't forget that it will keep living within us. That was why I felt that, in this instance, we had to go beyond tradition and make a needed exception.

This law was doing no more than insisting upon what I had already found just made good sense: that the most effective way to prevent a sex offender from repeating his crime is by making him known to all those around him so that they may become his *guardians.*

As far as I could see, that law had two benefits: it protected the public from sex offenders by letting the public know who we are, and it protected us from ourselves by reminding us of who we have been—every time we go into a police station to register—so that we don't become that kind of person again.

Megan's Law doesn't send police out to our homes to round us up and take us in to register. Instead, it puts the responsibility of registering on us, as it should in a democracy. And that makes it the most gentle deterrent that anyone could design.

Those who want to claim that, by its permanent display of our criminal records, *Megan's Law* compels us to wear a *Scarlet Letter* would be best advised to read Nathaniel Hawthorne's classic novel of that same name. Like us, his main character, Hester Prynne, was found guilty of a sex crime—adultery. Like us, she was required to let her community know the nature of her crime (by being forced to wear a large letter "A" of scarlet material on her dress). Like us, she had to do that for the rest of her life.

Undoubtedly, everyone expected her to flee rather than bear such a punishment. But, to their surprise, Hester not only wore the letter and remained there, she also accepted her punishment as a call to walk a path of penance and did so, being of service to anyone suffering from misfortune. In time, women in particular turned to her for counsel and, well before the end of her days, Hester Prynne succeeded in taking what had been meant as a 'badge of shame' and transforming it into a badge of service that brought her respect from all.

Not a bad idea. And perhaps that's why a sex offender registration and notification law now exists—in one form of another—not only in the United States, but in eight other countries as of this writing:

Australia
Canada
Ireland
Republic of Korea, and
United Kingdom of England, Wales, Northern Ireland and Scotland.

In two of those countries—Australia and Ireland—anyone who is already a registered sex offender in their home country must also register there when arriving as a tourist, if they plan to remain beyond a certain number of days. Other countries may follow suit. Sex Offender Registration laws are in the world to stay, whether they are called Megan's Law (U.S.), Christopher's Law (Canada), Sarah's Law (United Kingdom) or something else.

In response to my first two interviews, the media suggested I write the story of my recovery and that is when the present book began again. For those who continue to believe that Megan's Law is wrong, my advice has been steadfastly the same. If you don't like Megan's Law, overcome it by becoming Megan's Law: tell people yourself about your past.

Americans are the most forgiving people in the world—if you trust them first. But if you don't, and they find out about you on their own, they cannot be blamed if they also wonder what else you may be hiding.

Taking Vows

Two years after coming back from living abroad I joined a local meditation group. Several months later, its members invited me to take the same first vows given to every monk in that religion (*jukai*).

I wanted to do so very much but, in keeping with my new rule, I couldn't unless I first made sure the organization's leadership knew about my past. I asked the Zen Buddhist priest who was sponsoring me to be certain to tell the group's teacher.

He promised to do so, and I added: "Please be sure he knows that if, after learning of it, he changes his mind about my being given vows, I'll certainly understand."

He said he would do so and phone me afterwards.

"Well?" I asked, on the day he called back. "Did you tell him?"

"Yes, I did," said my friend.

"What did he say?"

"He said that he couldn't think of anyone who needed vows more."

The ceremony took place in a northern California redwood forest, where we went to meditate for a week. Late on the final night, all those there as candidates like myself were examined by our teacher to make sure our understanding of the vows we were about to take was sufficient. Afterwards, our vows were accepted and we donned the prayer shawls given out in memorial of the occasion.

After the ceremony, I was standing under some pine trees with my new 'dharma brothers and sisters,' as we called ourselves, when several of the senior monks came up to me along with my sponsor and asked me to step to one side with them.

"Yes?" I asked, after bowing to all of them first.

"We congratulate you," the most senior of them said. "You have now taken vows to spend the rest of your life helping others to overcome suffering. That is very good."

"However," my sponsor added. "There is one more vow we'd like you to take."

"Certainly," I said.

"Your extra vow must be to help all those injured by sexual abuse."

The senior monk added, "Consider that your 'special' beat. We'll take care of all the others."

I agreed, and that was how I was given the mission I carry out now.

Practicing My Vows

Upon my return to San Francisco, one of the news organizations informed me that, while I was in my part of the forest, a local sex offender went into another part of it and hung himself, apparently in shame after police distributed his photo in the nearby community.

"Some people are blaming the police for having 'hounded' the man to his death," said the reporter. "Would you agree?"

"Absolutely not," I replied. "The police were only doing their job, as the law permits them to tell people about those of us they consider to be 'most likely' to offend again. The man need not have killed himself and, had he told his neighbors himself about his past, he would not have felt that he had to do so."

I had just done the same thing. The police could have distributed my photo. I'd told them I was there, as required, since it was another county than my own. They, lawfully, could have put my photo up throughout the area. Knowing this, it only made good sense to let the leadership of my new religious organization be aware of my past; if police chose to publish it, the organization would be prepared to handle it.

Anyone else can do the same. And should. For that reason, as the first expression of my new vow, I began a prison outreach project, writing to convicted sex offenders in penitentiaries all over the country. Letting them know that my past was no different than theirs, I urged all of them to seek counseling and study themselves, so they can begin work on their recovery before they are released.

I also put up a Web site for those already in the community, explaining the many details of my state's version of Megan's Law (www.calsexoffenders.net). Writing as one of them, I encouraged them to obey this law and use it to help remain self-controlled. Later, I expanded the site to include a list of recovery resources, worldwide, for anyone seeking help in dealing with sexual compulsions.

Subsequently, I included a crisis counseling page for those who had lost control, committed the very worst of crimes, and now were in hiding as fugitives. Having been close to that myself at one point, I sought to call these men back by telling them how they could get legal help and arrange their safe surrender to police. Only in this way, I told them, could they be certain of being left with a life they could still restore.

It worked better than I could have hoped. When a wave of child kidnappings and murders broke out across the country, one man used the site's e-mail link to confess he had similar deadly urges toward little girls and wondered if I could help get him into a counseling group. With the aid of several national referral organizations and local therapists, the man was given two qualified clinicians within twenty-four hours.

The following year, I was invited to an international conference in the United Kingdom where I was permitted to facilitate dialogue groups for former victims of sexual abuse, standing openly among them as a former abuser.

Every convicted sexual offender can make a similar effort if he or she is willing to do so.

Cutting Through the Mountain

I wanted to find my now-adult daughter and at least offer her an apology. But no one in my family knew where she lived. Right after I went to prison, her family broke off all contact with mine and no one ever heard from them again. When I got back, and had a lawyer tell my ex-wife's attorney that I was willing to resume child support payments, my offer was declined, leaving me without any way of knowing where they might be now.

Several years later, while in town between trips abroad, I ran into a mutual friend who told me that he had seen my ex-wife. "She invited me over to see your daughter."

"Really?" But, before I could ask further, he said that the visit had been cancelled at the last minute. "She called back the next day and said they were still living with your ex-wife's mother, who refuses to let your daughter meet *anyone* who has ever known you."

That was then. Now my daughter was an adult and could be living anywhere. The only way to find her would be to have an attorney hire a private investigator to locate her.

Since I wasn't comfortable doing that, I sought the advice of several women I knew who had been sexually abused as children themselves. They all opposed the idea of trying to locate my daughter.

"You'd be re-victimizing her," they said, "by invading her privacy."

I agreed. As a rape counselor put it to me: "If she's over 18 and hasn't tried to contact you, *she doesn't want to hear from you.*"

It may have been just as well, for when I looked deeper within myself what I found was that what I wanted was not only to apologize to my daughter but also to seek her forgiveness.

That's not her job to give. Finding it, if possible, is mine.

Perhaps, if I continue my work and she hears of it, she may choose to send me a signal that my approach would be welcome. And, perhaps not. As I have written to several prisoners with whom I now correspond, "not being forgiven may be part of the punishment we have drawn down upon ourselves. That doesn't mean it has to end there. While we may never attain forgiveness, this might help us to become more forgiving of others when they ask it of us."

What do you do, then, when you are left with a debt to pay and no one who can accept payment? The answer was found by another man, three centuries ago in Japan. He was a notorious highwayman of that day who had robbed and killed many. Finally, on one moonlit night, as he looked down on the bodies of his newest victims he was shocked to find that, this time, they were a young bride and groom, barely older than children.

"What have I done?" he asked himself in horror. All the ugliness of his life stared back up at him.

"I must pay for what I've done" he said to himself and began walking all the way to Tokyo to surrender himself.

Knowing that his execution would be immediate, the moment he saw a small Buddhist temple outside of town he thought to himself, "Since I will be meeting The Buddha today, I might as well do so with clean hands," and asked to see a priest to make his confession.

An old monk was summoned and the man told him of all that he had done, as well as his intention to surrender to authorities now.

But, to his surprise, the old monk didn't give him the forgiveness he had expected. Instead, the old monk asked him: "Why do you want to *cheat* the Buddha? By your own account, you have taken many lives. Now, you propose to pay for this by giving back only one—your own."

Startled, the man replied, "But that's all I have!"

"No," said the priest. "Instead of rushing to the executioner, you could stay here, train to become a monk and spend the rest of your days out on the highway saving others from men like you. That is how you could pay The Buddha for all that you have taken."

The man did so, eventually becoming the "Saint Christopher" of Japan—its patron saint for travelers. It's a true story and guides what I do with my life now.

Here's what any former offender can also do if he wants to earn his way back into the community:

The Ten Commandments for a Recovering Sex Offender

1. Overcome the Destructive Side of Yourself

We are people who have done terrible things. We have grievously injured many, some perhaps for the rest of their lives. If we do not grasp these facts—and do not have any feeling of sorrow for our victims—there is no way we can ever return to the community and be accepted by it. Remorse is the first step toward community reintegration.

That's not to say that we should bury ourselves in a shame so deep that it discourages us from believing we can ever be anything other than what we have been. All too often, shame alone does nothing more than leave us wallowing in self-pity, which is useless. Don't let your focus be on yourself, but on others, and allow yourself to have a strong and permanent sense of abiding regret—not for what's happened to you, but to them because of you. For that regret, which others call remorse, will become the first wall in keeping you from ever harming anyone else again

See yourself now as you are: as a person instead of just as a person ruled by an urge. Be more than an 'offender.' Think of yourself, instead, as someone whose life has given them an enormous opportunity to become heroic by overcoming the destructive side of your self.

Live like a warrior and tame yourself by respecting the power of your sexual urges. Never let yourself go into the world with urges that are still gathering power.

2. Choose your associates carefully so that you aren't mentally contaminated by them.

We become part of everyone with whom we travel and the sum of every journey we take. Choose where you go carefully and with whom you wish to sojourn, for by the end of the journey each of you will be a part of the other.

If you allow yourself to fall back into the same old haunts and return to running around with the same kind of people to play the same old games as you did before you were convicted, it is as certain as tomorrow's sunrise that you will be convicted again.

Associate with people who inspire you to have a richer life.

3. Behave only as a guest in the community and not as one of its equals. Respect not just its laws, but its sensitivities.

If you are a convicted rapist, don't believe that you have a 'right' to go to the same running trails that women use. If you are a convicted child molester and there's a park near your residence where children play, make a voluntary sacrifice and find another park. Don't insist upon living right next door to families with children or in predominantly-family neighborhoods. They don't want you there and it only needlessly tempts you to be there.

This is not the time to test your new strength at the expense of the community's fears. For now, just content yourself with earning its toleration of your presence. Acceptance will come later. Don't try to force people into welcoming you by imposing yourself on them.

4. Practice self-disclosure about your past.

Don't be afraid to tell people about your past. You'll be thanked for doing so, if you do it humbly and with some sense of regret. Human beings are amazingly forgiving if you are willing to trust them and they are forever suspicious if they find out about you on their own.

You don't have to tell everyone. Just tell those who offer the hand of friendship. Any time you realize that a person is about to go from being an acquaintance to becoming a friend, ask them to pause a moment. Tell them how much you appreciate their company. Then, confess that, out of respect for them, there is something you must tell them about your past that they have a right to know. Assure them that if, after they've heard it, they don't want to associate with you anymore, you'll respect their right not to do so.

Then, in the simplest possible terms, tell them about your past. For example: "A number of years ago (whenever) I did something that I regret very much. I (molested a child/forced a woman, etc). I've been convicted for it, as I should have been. Since that time, I've been in counseling (or "I'm now in counseling") so that it never happens again. I regret it ever happened and I seek to live a much better life now. But I felt that you had a right to know about it. Thank you for hearing me out."

I have never yet been rejected by anyone to whom I have made such a disclosure and, instead, am able to count on them as members of an ever-widening support group within my community that encourages my continued recovery.

You can do the same and never have to fear that others are going to find out about you on their own.

5. Respect the law: stay registered.

Registration protects us as well as the community. It keeps the community safe by letting others know who we are, and it keeps us safe by reminding us of who we have been so that we don't become that kind of person again.

Its alternatives are not better. Calls have already been heard, in this country and abroad, to have all convicted sex offenders confined in the same place, far away from the community, in special camps of their own from which they could never leave.

It's called *preventative detention* and it could be done. At the beginning of World War II, the United States forced over 100,000 of its Japanese-born American citizens into "relocation camps." Don't think it couldn't happen again.

You have the power to prevent that. Every time you walk into a police station to register or re-register, you are casting another vote against preventative detention by demonstrating that you are a law-abiding person who doesn't need to be confined.

6. Keep healing.

"…maintenance is forever."

Marques, J.K., Murrey, C.L. and O'Connor, D.M., AN INNO-VATIVE TREATMENT PROGRAM FOR SEX OFFENDERS Report to the Legislature in Response to 1983/84 Budget Act Item 4440-011-001, State of California.

According to the most accurate figures currently available, therapy for sex offenders wears off over time. This suggests it's to our own benefit to remain in some kind of permanent maintenance program. A list of national and international organizations for sexual addicts that offers self-recovery programs appears below. Use them, or counseling programs equivalent to them. Consciousness is all we've got. Taking care of it is our highest calling.

7. Make amends to your victims except when doing so would harm them or others.

Unless they have made it clear that they do not wish to hear from you, have your former victims contacted through a trustworthy third party—e.g. your minister or legal representative—and given a letter of apology from you.

Leave it to your former victims to decide if they would like to meet with you to discuss what happened in the past.

If they choose to permit a meeting, use a professional victim/offender mediator if you can (such as those available through the recognized organizations listed under Websites in the Readers' Resources section in the back of this book) so that the meeting may be one where the risk is minimal that either of you will be injured further by it.

Prepare yourself to express your regret, your sense of responsibility for what you did and your concern for your victim's future well being.

Do whatever you can to contribute to their further healing. But do not look to them to gain a forgiveness you can only earn by yourself by serving many others over a long period of time.

If your victim does not want to meet with you, leave them in peace for that is making amends to them too.

8. Cooperate with your community and work with your neighbors.

Be willing to participate in any community meeting about you to which you are invited and, when attending, be honest, polite and courteous in your response to any question you may be asked.

Understand that many people will be as afraid of you as you are of them. Be prepared to answer their concerns about you. Be open and willing to remain accountable to them whenever you encounter any of them in your daily life.

No matter how angry or hurt any of them may be (for some of them may also be former victims of sexual abuse by others), accept them as your guardians, for it is their watchfulness that will cause you to be watchful about yourself. And that is what will keep you out of prison.

9. Forgive anyone who has ever abused you and become a lamp of forgiveness to the entire community.

In every tragedy, life is always asking us one question: "Do you still love me?" Like it or not, life is our lover and if we will not forgive what she sometimes does to us her name is Hell.

Were I to meet-up again with the person who first molested me, I would neither sue nor prosecute him, for that would only make him a burden on his family.

I do not consider myself his "victim." I consider myself as having been the recipient of a damaging process that came through him after beginning a long, long time before he ever came into my life.

Were I to encounter him again, I would say nothing about our past unless he was now in a position to harm others, in which case I would then report him. For victims who only seek vengeance become abusers themselves and you cannot fix your own life by wrecking anyone else's.

10. Establish sexual government

Know what triggers your offending and outwit it. If you feel lonely, find the joy of being with yourself. If you are feeling low, ask yourself why you think your life should be the only one not to have any suffering in it.

Avoid situations of known temptation and have escape strategies in place when they occur. Accept as fact that urges to act inappropriately come to everyone; don't fear such urges. All it takes to establish sexual government is remembering that, before there's an urge, there's a self to hear it.

Be that self. For, so long as you remain self-governing, no one else shall govern you.

*   *   *

How to Protect Your Children

1. Teach your children that they don't have to accept "dares" to prove to anyone else that they are brave.
2. Teach your children that sex for money is not okay because it is not theirs to sell, but a sacred power they have been given by life itself.
3. Teach your children not to use their sexual attractiveness to get the attention of anyone they know they cannot handle yet.
4. Teach your children that, if anyone tells them they are a registered sex offender, the most appropriate response is to say, "Thank you for telling me. I rely on you to stay in recovery."

5. Teach your children to choose carefully with whom they associate (including when on the Internet), so they do not fall under the influence of others who do not have any self-respect.

6. Teach your children to practice sexual self-government themselves so they may rule their own biological urges responsibly.

*　　　　　*　　　　　*

Questions to Consider

1. Johns Hopkins' Dr. Fred Berlin says that, since sex offenders don't choose their sexual inclinations any more than anyone else does, it isn't fair to 'blame' them, but it is fair to insist that they be responsible for governing themselves. What do you think?

2. What would be an appropriate occupation for a person previously convicted of a sexual offense?

3. Was it better that the former highwayman became a monk, spending the rest of his days saving others, or do you think that he should have been executed?

4. Under what circumstances, if any, should a convicted sex offender be spared imprisonment? And, if so, what should he be ordered to do to atone for his crime?

Chapter Ten

The Healing of America

Overcoming superstition

There are certain misconceptions about sex offenders that the public and its policymakers will have to overcome if the problem of sex offending is ever to be solved. The first of these lies in the term itself: *sex offender*. There are two kinds: the active sex offender who is continuing to commit crimes and the *former* sex offender, who stopped doing so. Those who fail to separate them will needlessly frighten themselves by overly-magnifying the problem. It is possible that up to eighty percent of all those listed as 'sex offenders' on state websites are people who stopped offending some time ago. That makes them 'former' sex offenders.

Even among the active sex offenders, very few are as dangerous as those who get the most publicity and use violence to get their victims. A recent portrait compiled by the Minnesota Department of Corrections revealed that the typical victim of sexual assault is a female under the age of eighteen years who is usually an acquaintance or relative of the offender and not a victim seized in some dark alley.

Half the time she turns out to have been living with her abuser.

A later report issued by the nation's leading organization of clinicians in this field finds no ground for viewing *all* sex offenders as dangerous. It is a "misconception," the organization writes, "that *all* sex offenders are highly likely to commit new sex offenses, and…most sex offenses against children are committed, not by strangers, but by *family members and others the child knows and trusts.*"

British police echo those same findings:

> *Within the UK, all research and crime statistics reveal that in excess of 80% of sexual offences committed against children are perpetrated by family members of the child.*
>
> *In approximately 10-12% of other cases the offender was known to the child and occupied a position of trust, i.e. a member of the clergy, a teacher, a sports coach, etc.*
>
> *In only 1 or 2% of cases is the child abused or attacked by someone unknown to them...*

—Letter to Mr. R.J. Goldenflame, JD MA, dated 13 September 1999 from Inspector Ian P. Clark, Staff Officer to the Chief Constable, Gloucestershire Constabulary, England.

According to one of the top experts in this field, the truly dangerous sex offenders are no more numerous than the dangerous lunatics of all other kinds, such as mass murderers: two to five percent at most. (Anna C. Salter, *PREDATORS: Pedophiles, Rapists and Other Sex Offenders* (New York, 2003) p. 97.)

Contrary to popular myth, sex offender recidivism rates are not out of control. According to figures for child molesters released by the United States Department of Justice in 2004, in the first three years following imprisonment it's only 3.3%, compared to almost 70% for all other kinds of released prisoners. According to Canadian research officials, over the long-term, over half of all convicted sex offenders do not re-offend.

Failing to recognize these facts, the nation has increasingly shifted away from neighborhood control of sex offenders through use of *Megan's Law* and toward more vengeance-driven policies. Thanks to poorly-written Internet websites created by the states, the rise of vigilante commentators in the media, and irresponsible political officeholders trying only to inflame the voters rather than enlighten them, broad parts of the nation have turned away from accepting the convicted offender of yesterday in their midst. Viewing all offenders as if they were only the worst of them, many in the electorate now favor:

- vastly increased prison sentences
- the mandatory use of Global Positioning System devices strapped onto the former offender for life to monitor his every location, and
- new laws that take away the homes of those who registered and banish them from the cities forever.

According to corrections officials and academics investigating these strategies, none of them work. Instead of reducing child sex offending, they are seen only as more likely to increase it:

—According to a Canadian government study of the effect of longer prison sentences, they don't discourage criminals: "...harsher criminal justice sanctions had no deterrent effect on recidivism. On the contrary, punishment produced a slight (3%) increase in recidivism."

—According to a California sex offender treatment organization looking at monitoring convicted sex offenders by electronic surveillance technology, rather than protecting children, widespread reliance on devices such as the Global Positioning Satellite system were found to be far more likely only to lull the public into a false sense of security as these only record the *location* of the former offender and not a thing about what he may be doing there.

—As Florida researchers found, moving those who registered to rural areas led only to their homelessness, or new residences too distant to reach, preventing them from receiving the close supervision they were supposed to be given to enhance public safety.

There may even be harsher consequences. Every week, I receive letters from convicted sex offenders in prisons all over the country. I've been hearing from them since I began my prison outreach project eight years ago and I encourage them to make their prison experience as positive a process as possible.

In the face of new laws that would forbid many of them from coming back—at least to the cities, where most of them have family and support services upon which they will need to rely—I'm now hearing anger and, in some cases, rage. They went to prison, believing they would get a chance at a new life when they got out. Now, when it appears this may not be so, some are threatening violence.

"We'll kill their children first!"

Men write, telling me how the older convicted child molesters in their yard are openly encouraging the younger ones to kill the victims next time, rather than chance getting caught under new laws that would never let them out again.

As I've warned members of Congress who are putting the finishing touches on a proposed National Sex Offender Registration law, we could have an insurgency right here, with children as its casualties.

Flawed State Websites

Internet publication of state sex offender registries that only give enough information to scare you, but not enough to allow you to protect yourself and your family, must improve. Throwing thousands of 'mug shots' at viewers, without providing all the information people need in order to decide for themselves what precautions are necessary, only plays to the 'fear' vote.

Instead of using highly technical legal terms that not even a lawyer from another state would understand, state websites should tell you the name of the crime of which the registrant was convicted *in plain English*: Rape, Child Molestation, etc. Not "Sexual Assault in the Third Degree," which doesn't mean a thing unless you've got a copy of that state's penal code and know how to read it. The website for Washington, D.C. does a far better job of calling the crimes by names most people can understand. Its lead should be followed.

When did the person commit their crime? Was it six months ago, in which case you would be justified in keeping a close watch over someone like that living near your home. Or was it *forty years ago*, in which case you can probably relax as that person obviously knows how to live a self-controlled life.

We have websites with people on them whose convictions are just that old who have never re-offended. States aren't telling you this, and as a result they are not telling you that many, if not most, of the people listed are only *former* offenders. Surveying the sites of several states, it appears that up to 80% of the people listed long ago finished being on parole or probation and have never been convicted of a sex offense again. You should be given each person's date of conviction so you can see for yourself how long ago their last sex offense was committed.

These sites should also tell who you can telephone, in your own community, if you are concerned about any of the people listed on these registries, such as the name and office telephone number of their parole agent or probation officer. Or the name and telephone number of the sexual assault police officer in your precinct for all those who don't fall under such supervision. This information should be there so that you may prevent crimes instead of just being made to wait until more of them happen.

Beware of "Risk Levels," given by some state websites for each person listed; they are only *estimates* of what someone may do and not predictions. Just as a life insurance company can predict how many people of your age will die in a certain number of years—but not whether you will be one of them—it is now possible to predict how many people convicted of the same crime are likely to commit another, but not *who*. Thus it is misleading to call all former offenders "Level I offenders" or "Level II offenders" or "Level III offenders," as if each was equally likely to re-offend. Only some are.

It is presently impossible to say who will re-offend, no matter what label they are given or in what "risk level" they are placed. On the basis of my own background, a risk level would say that I should have re-offended. But I haven't done so and I'm now completing my fifteenth year since leaving prison.

So much for estimates; that's all they are. They should be used as guides: be more careful with people in higher risk levels. But don't make the mistake of thinking that they are certain to re-offend. Nothing could be more mistaken. It's just a well-meant note of caution from your police, and nothing more. Give the man a chance to prove himself. In Washington State, calling some former offenders 'Level III' led to the murder of two of them, allegedly by a vigilante who mistakenly believed that "Level III" meant these men were definitely going to re-offend. Within hours, convicted sex offenders across the country were arming themselves, an excellent example of how easy it is for hysteria to take root on both sides.

Vigilante Commentators

Vigilante commentators have done us no good either. Instead of telling us how we can reform the offenders we have caught, they seem intent only on trying to whip their audiences into lynch-mob hysteria. Endlessly preaching longer sentences, tougher laws and no tolerance for anything that might solve the problem of sex offending, they are more responsible than anyone else for the fact that many of the new proposals now being considered are also the ones most likely to backfire. It's your children who will pay the price if they prevail.

This is not meant as an indictment of conservative commentators. Some of the best commentators we have are conservative. It is an indictment of extremists.

Listen to other commentators. Do what the best news reporters do and read some books on the subject. Don't forget that the media is in business to make money, and that it can't make enough money unless it attracts a lot of viewers, listeners or readers. This forces it to give first place to the stories that grab our attention instead of to those that may be more enlightening. This is why you always hear about the previously-convicted sex offender who gets arrested again, but never about the one who just successfully completed his parole.

The media is not a university, only a community bulletin board alerting you to issues that call for your closer attention.

Inflammatory Politicians

Many of our office holders have not provided the most responsible leadership. In support of one measure pending Congressional approval at the time of this writing, its sponsors wrote an article calling all those convicted of any sexual offense "predators, pedophiles and criminals."

To suggest that a person arrested for indecent exposure is a "predator" only mocks the term. A *pedophile* means someone whose sexual offense was against a child below a certain age, and that only applies to some who have been convicted and not others. People who have already paid for their crime and gone on to live a law-abiding life for years deserve far better than to be called "criminals" today.

This kind of language does not encourage others to recover, which is what the country needs.

Even more important, some of the legislation that has been proposed doesn't even go after 'sex offenders' as much as 'former sex offenders' who are no threat.

To falsely suggest that a 'sex offender' is living down the street from you, when he is really a *former* sex offender convicted decades ago and never since, only needlessly frightens your family. It is inflammatory politics and has you looking at people who haven't done anything in years instead of watching out for the predator on the Internet who is coming into your child's bedroom through her computer tonight.

Another member of Congress had his bill call *all* sex offenders "violent sexual predators," which no responsible clinician or treatment provider would support. Lawmakers who seek only to burden those who obey the law and register, rather than go after the ones who don't, are not serving your children's best interests. Vote for better candidates who use intelligence instead of playing to the "fear" vote.

A lot of "law and order" candidates get money from the prison construction industry or prison guards unions. Normally, there would be nothing to criticize about that. But these are not 'normal' times any longer: convicted sex offenders in prisons across the country are telling us that they will kill the children next time if laws become any more harsh.

We cannot afford to keep people in public office who are raising penalties just to get a campaign contribution when it could cost us our children.

Saving *Megan's Law*

Megan's Law is all we need to establish neighborhood control over convicted sex offenders. If we turn away from it and banish all those from the cities who have obeyed it, there is no guarantee they will register again and we could wind up exactly where we were before Megan's Law was enacted.

Yes, that means sometimes you are going to have people around who you would really rather not have around; it's part of the unpleasantness of life. But it's better than not knowing where they are at all. Taking away their homes just so they don't live "near" a school—instead of just making it a crime for them to step on school property—could wind up having them living in the alley behind your home without your even knowing they are there. Don't vote for such foolish laws.

Use Megan's Law to protect yourself and your family by going to your state's sex offender registry and checking on anyone you would:

- Date
- Marry
- Go into business with
- Work for
- Hire, or
- Use to take care of your children. (Even your relatives. Especially your relatives. Most sex offenses are committed by family members or people who are close to your child. If you have a nephew or uncle who has been convicted, he's not likely to tell you about it and it would be reckless for you to leave your child with him.)
- You can use it to look up new neighbors, for the safety of your family.

The Supreme Court of the United States has now said that it is everyone's constitutional right to look up convicted sex offenders. Don't wait for the police to come to your door to tell you that there's a new registrant living in your neighborhood. Police have too many doors to come to and by the time they get to yours it could be too late.

Remember to use your own judgment. Megan's Law won't—and can't—tell you who was really innocent and wrongly convicted but still has to register under it.

I've received several e-mails suggesting that's happened. One man told of how, after spending 67 days in a brutal county jail, he accepted an offer from the prosecutor to get out by admitting guilt to what he thought was a minor sexual offense. Now, he finds, he must register for the rest of his life as a *convicted sex offender.*

The same thing happened to another man facing a prison sentence so horrendously long that he feared to take a chance and go through trial. He had a family to support and couldn't place them in jeopardy by risking such a fate.

Some people just lost their case! They weren't guilty. It's just that their attorney didn't do as well as the prosecutor. It happens in courtrooms all the time, in all kinds of cases.

That's not to say that everyone listed under the registration law is innocent, or even that most of them are not guilty. What it does say is that this list is just a start. Don't assume anything just because you've found someone who is on it. If the person is someone who is trying to get close to your family, tell them that you found them listed on the sex offender registry and see what kind of a response they give you. In almost all cases, they'll simply admit it. If they insist they weren't guilty, you'll have to use your own judgment as to whether you can believe them or not.

If someone on this list is living near you, phone the police and ask them to tell you who his community supervisor is (his parole agent or probation officer) and ask for their phone number. Then phone them and ask them to tell you how he committed the crime(s) for which he is registered, so you know what to look out for. If he doesn't have a community supervisor, ask the police to help you get this information. It could save your child's life.

Community Outreach Efforts

See if you can get your church or house of worship to start looking in on former offenders residing in your community. A religious group up in Canada did so and accomplished miracles.

It was almost a decade ago when the Mennonite religious order decided to help heal sex offenders themselves. Taking their stand in Radical Christianity, they said that if, in His time, Jesus healed lepers (the social outcasts of His era), Christians should help heal sex offenders today.

Their first attempt to do so was with a high-risk 54-year old child molester about to leave prison after his eighth conviction. They met with his caseworker, agreed to help the man find a place to stay, a job and build a new circle of friends who would support his living a new life. Then they contacted the police to let them know of their involvement.

Detectives were not overjoyed at the news. "We didn't want him here."

The moment he arrived in the community, his picture was made available to the media and the public warned of his presence.

Irate parents began picketing and the Mennonites received so many angry phone calls that, for the first time in their lives, they had to buy a telephone answering machine.

The police intensified their surveillance, certain the man would quickly re-offend.

A neighbor phoned, who had small children and was very concerned for their safety. They invited her to come over and tell the man her fears so that he could speak to them. Several other neighbors were also invited, as were the police.

Ground rules were quickly established. Everyone would sit in a circle and speak one at a time, followed by an opportunity for the man to respond. He was asked a number of questions:

- why had he been in prison?
- what was his sentence?
- what treatment had he obtained?
- what treatment did he plan to get now that he was out of prison?

Other participants asked him the best way he had learned to avoid repeating his misconduct, and how he planned to deal with the anger that some people might feel toward him.

He answered each question fully and respectfully and tensions began to ease.

A program was set up by which he would be contacted every day by at least one member of a small group of Mennonite volunteers who would check on how he was doing. He was given help in finding furniture and an apartment while police met regularly with the organization and began acting as a buffer between the man and the community, correcting rumors and preventing problems.

The man's life soon settled into a comfortable pattern as he took up residence in his own apartment and developed some close relationships among a small network of people willing to encourage him to remain self-controlled.

As a result of this experience, the Mennonites found themselves with a model they could use with other men like him and now do so regularly. Each man works with a small group of volunteers who learn about sexual deviation, its damage to victims and the prospects for recovery by both victim and offender before serving for one year.

A formal agreement is set up between the man and his group by which he agrees to accept their help and advice, pursue appropriate treatment and act responsibly in the community. In return, volunteers agree to help him. Procedures are established for failure to live up to these commitments, with consequences that can include adjustment of terms or, when necessary, withdrawal of support and notification of authorities.

Former victims who have processed their experience well are also invited to some meetings so that their needs and views are addressed, too.

First statistics on the program's results show that these men do *twice* as well as men who are not in this program and that, when new crimes are committed by them, they are substantially less severe than the offense for which they had previously been imprisoned.

Says one Canadian Correctional Services official:

"I fundamentally believe sex offenders are a problem of the community that needs to be addressed by the community. If you wait for politicians and government bureaucrats to do it, there are going to be far too many abused children because there aren't enough of us."

—Robin J. Wilson, director of the Sexual Behavior Program, Canadian Correctional Service, quoted by Journalist Candis McLean in her article "Next step—a national registry," REPORT NEWSMAGAZINE, June 3, 2002, Alberta, Canada

Your congregation could do the same thing. Your minister or priest or rabbi could get help from local community corrections agencies—the Probation Department, State Parole, local police—and reach out to those registered individuals in your community to help them stay in recovery.

Look what happened in my own case when the Buddhists picked me up! Nothing encourages a former offender to remain 'former' more than a community that encourages him to do so.

Speak to other members of your congregation and its pastor and ask them to help if only because the problem of sex offenders in the community isn't likely to go away by itself.

More are Coming

According to two of the founders of modern-day sex offender therapy, more people find children erotically appealing than is widely acknowledged. Writing in their classic work, *Handbook of Sexual Assault*, Canada's W.L. Marshall and H.E. Barbaree suggest that at least *one out of every six men demonstrate significant levels of erotic arousal to girls as young as age thirteen*.

Rape statistics are similarly alarming. According to one of the newest books on the subject, *one out of every three college-age men admitted they would force a woman to have sex with them if they were certain that they could get away with it*. (Malamouth 1989; Young and Thiessen 1991, cited in

Thornhill and Palmer, *A NATURAL HISTORY OF RAPE,* Cambridge 2000 at p. 77)

What these findings indicate is that there will always be sex offenders. They will continue to come forth in every generation. Locking them all up and throwing away the key is not the answer, for that would not reach those who have not yet been born. And when *they* come forth, knowing that is all you're going to do with them, the likelihood is that they will feel the same way that some already do now. As sex offender Psychologist Anna C. Salter writes of a typical serial rapist, "The threat of jail only made him consider killing his victim."

Any of them could become a *Man with Nothing Left to Lose* and that is a danger we dare not create when there are far better alternatives. Children in danger of becoming sexual predators can be identified and helped before it's too late. Juveniles as well as adults who begin to offend can be given treatment to stop their offending. Those who have already become career sex offenders can be caught and prosecuted and treated while in prison.

What we need to do is catch them, confine them and then heal them.

People who commit sex offenses against children should be given a life sentence, with treatment made available to them from Day One of their sentence.

They should not get out until their treatment team says they are ready.

They should be closely monitored when they return to the community—preferably in a group home under appropriate supervision, situated far away from family neighborhoods.

If they so much as 'look' funny, they can be returned to prison for the rest of their life sentence.

Only after they have been back in the community under these conditions for several years—without having had any problems—should be they be released completely, and then kept under Megan's Law.

A prison chaplain should be made available to every sex offender who wants to use one. Adding a spiritual dimension to recovery strengthens it enormously.

Sentences shouldn't stop with prison. Every convicted sex offender who returns to the community should be required to do *community service* as part of his payment to society for having damaged it. All but those deemed sadistic offenders should be required to appear before victims groups so that they can tell him how much damage his kind of acts really caused. Very few offenders ever find out. Is it any wonder that they don't have any remorse? They have never seen any of the long-term consequences of what they've done and should be made to do so.

Demand these changes. Tell your state legislators that you want them.

Critics may complain that all of this will cost too much money. But it is a lot less expensive than years in prison and then another new victim when they get out, which is all we are doing now.

Let Judges Determine Punishments, not Politicians.

For too many years now, politicians have tried to say that judges are too lenient. As a result, many laws have been passed that tie a judge's hands and force the court to hand down a sentence written in advance in a statute. Every individual deserves to be judged solely on the basis of his own case. The alternative is lynch mob justice and that only serves to make criminals more desperate not to get caught.

Courts were created so that their judges could restrain us from letting our passions—instead of wisdom—govern. They were made independent so they could even restrain the legislature from acting excessively. They were created as the guardians of our reason. Don't let politicians who appeal only to anger determine what justice is to be or we will be devoured by violence.

Let judges judge. Call some of them up and ask to meet them in court with your neighbors during a recess. Have them tell you what they think should be done in sex offense cases. You may be surprised at the variety of opinions they have.

If you are satisfied with what you've heard, tell your local and national legislators that *you want judges left free to judge.* If you don't like what a judge does, you can always elect another.

There is no such thing as an easy answer to complex problems. A comprehensive plan is what is needed; with different prescriptions for different

kinds of people: halfway houses for those on parole, a continuing maintenance program afterwards with peer-led monitoring, registration and
community notification so that neighbors can guard their families, and a
willingness on the nation's part to let former offenders heal instead of seeing them used only as distractions from the nation's other problems.

The nation itself will heal as a result. It is already beginning to do so.

The Healing of America

The healing of America can be found in Fargo, North Dakota. That was
where the last suspected serial child molester lived before he went down
the highway to Idaho and allegedly massacred an entire family. The day
after he was apprehended, I was telephoned by Fargo's WDAY Talkradio
Network and invited to take calls from listeners there.

I expected to be facing a very hostile audience as these people had just
discovered that a man who had lived in their midst had now allegedly
committed some of the most horrible crimes anyone could imagine. Yet,
what I found when going on the air was that the community was 'search-
ing its heart' to ask itself if there wasn't 'something' that they might have
done, by reaching out to this man, that might have kept him from doing
what he had now been accused of doing.

It's that kind of courageous self-honesty that brings forth the Healing of
America.

There are two women I have the privilege of knowing who exemplify it,
too. Both have been victims of horrible sexual abuse. One was brutally
raped and the other has several children who were molested. Under these
circumstances, you might expect them to be seething with rage.

That is not to say they didn't feel anger at one time; they wouldn't be
human if they hadn't felt some very strong emotions after what had happened to them.

But they didn't stay there. They didn't make 'being a victim' their permanent identity. Like Marc Klaas, who I mentioned above, they got back
up and went on to do something that could heal this nation. Marc established a nationwide organization that helps law enforcement—and the

parents involved—when children are abducted (*The Polly Klaas Foundation*). He is a vigilant spokesman for victim's rights and strong, tough sentences, but not ones that are merely vengeful.

One of the two women, Jeri Elster (ChangeLaws@aol.com), became involved in lengthening the time within which sex offenders can be prosecuted when DNA evidence is available. Later, after spending years in treatment and counseling, she decided that the only way she could heal further would be by helping those like her offender to heal too. She has now been certified to work with convicted rapists in prison so that, like the first therapist who helped me, none of them comes back to hurt anyone else.

The other woman mentioned above has similarly gone on to volunteer in a community mental health project where she now helps registered sex offenders stay in recovery so that none of them lapse and molest anyone else's children.

That is what will heal America for, as I wrote above, whenever a sex offender harms another he also harms himself, leaving both his victim and himself wounded. From that time on, neither can be healed until both are healed, as it is one and the same wound.

We can only find our way back by helping those who have harmed others to find their way back, too. If we only seek to rescue ourselves while abandoning those who have done us harm, ultimately we'll be surrounded only by people who still want to harm us. That is not a national policy that any country should adopt.

There can be no child safety without offender reform, while keeping those locked up who won't reform.

This means we have to be willing to see more than only the worst in people; we have to be willing to see what else they can be, too. If we refuse to do so, it is we who deny any better future to ourselves.

It isn't going to be easy to get. Hate can be as seductive as sex. What we have to do is learn how to be more careful with both.

<u>60 Ways to Protect Your Children from Sexual Predators</u>

14 Steps You Can Take by Yourself

Make a sacred promise to yourself not to react in anger or distress if your child tells you that he or she was approached or touched inappropriately, or your child may be afraid to tell you.

Use Megan's Law to check on anyone you would use to take care of your children (even your relatives).

Use Megan's Law to check on new neighbors.

Use Megan's Law to check on anyone you would date, as they will be around your children.

Use Megan's Law to check on anyone you would marry.

Use Megan's Law to check on anyone you would go into business with, work for or hire, as they may also be around your child some time.

Never leave your child in a youth group that leaves any child alone with one adult instead of two and, preferably, of the opposite gender from each other.

Don't be an absent parent, not home on the weekends when your kids are going out, and always have a way they can reach you, wherever you are.

Don't go on vacation as a parent when you take your children with you on vacation, especially in a foreign country.

Don't allow your children to go off with any hotel or cruise ship employee unless there are at least two of them supervising the children, preferably one male and one female who are adults themselves, or go with them.

At home, encourage your children to tell you who their friends are, and their ages. If they are too much older, ask them to see them only in your home, when you can be around also.

Ask your children where they have been each day after school so you know where they are going and who they are seeing.

Make it your business to know any of your child's acquaintances or friends who are adults.

Warn your children that there are also children who have already been abused who may try to abuse them.

25 Ways to Arm Your Child Against Sexual Predators

Tell your child never to let any stranger into your home, no matter what government agency they claim to represent.

Teach your children never to go into any neighbor's home alone unless they have playmates there.

Teach your children not to hitchhike: in cars or on the Internet.

Tell your children never to go off alone with any adult unless it is someone you know, too, and you know where they are going and how they can be reached there.

Teach them to get away from any adult who starts talking to them about sex.

Don't let your daughter dress as if she is a woman until she becomes a woman, so that she doesn't attract what only a woman could handle, or you may get phoned by police to come down to the E.R. some night to find her.

Teach your children that they don't have to accept "dares" to prove they are brave to anyone.

Teach your older children that *oral sex* is sex, too.

Teach them that oral sex can also give them sexual illnesses.

Teach your children that the test to live by isn't 'how it feels' but how they would feel about themselves afterwards.

Teach them not to be the first to try anything they haven't learned about fully: like cigarettes with strange smells, drugs and so called "thriller" drinks. Some adolescents have been killed by these.

Give them a cell phone already programmed to dial 911 at the touch of a button whenever they are away from you.

Teach your children that their job is to take care of their lives by being careful where they go.

Teach your children to choose carefully with whom they associate (even on the Internet), so they do not fall under the influence of others who do not have any self-respect.

Teach your children that they have choices as to what happens to them and that they can ask you for help in making them.

Teach them the truth about life: that it can be dangerous, and that we *all* have the task of living carefully and not as if nothing can happen to us.

Teach your children that everything we do has consequences that cannot be avoided, so they must act carefully and with good sense.

Set limits to what your children do, how late they can stay out, and where they can go, and enforce those limits. Right now, you are their Guard Tower.

Teach them that sex is not a toy we are given, but a power that is sacred.

Teach them that sex for money is never okay.

Teach them to live modestly as there really is such a thing as going 'too far.' People don't come back from there.

Don't excuse them when they fail to stay within the limits you have set. Hold them accountable or their life will do so, the hard way.

Teach them that fear of the Lord—no matter how you define that term—is the beginning of wisdom, so they may stay protected by it.

Teach your children to rule their biological urges responsibly.

Teach them that if someone tells them he is a registered sex offender, the most appropriate thing to say is, "Thank you for telling me. I rely on you to stay in recovery."

11 Tasks You Can Have Your Government Do to Increase Your Children's Safety

Go to your state's Registered Sex Offenders website and if it:

—doesn't describe each person's crimes in plain English that you can understand;

—doesn't list each person's date of conviction so you know how long it's been since he last committed a sex offense, or

—doesn't tell you who you can contact (and their office phone number) in your own community, about anyone listed

write your state lawmakers and tell them you want them to have those items included.

Call the local office of your state lawmakers and of your members of Congress and ask them to tell you what ideas they have to protect children from sex offenders so that you may influence those ideas before they become law.

Tell your members of Congress and the state legislature that you want convicted sex offenders to be given sentences that include treatment before they are released or as a condition of that release.

Tell your members of Congress and the state legislature that you want sentences that leave a prisoner with a chance to come back into the community when he has earned it.

Don't let anyone try to convince you that all we have to do to stop sex offenders is have them castrated. The offender's problem isn't in his groin but in his mind.

Don't let anyone try to tell you that, because sex offending can't be "cured," a convicted offender can't be adequately trained to keep himself under control.

Don't let your legislators pass laws that would drive away former sex offenders living in recovery or you risk discouraging them from remaining in recovery or registering.

Tell your legislators that you want formerly convicted sex offenders to have a place where they can meet and be in an ongoing recovery group.

Don't let anyone convince you that convicted offenders meeting in approved maintenance groups will only waste their time there trying to figure out ways to find more victims. If you really have doubts about such a group, phone your local police and have them look into it for you.

Don't believe that convicted sex offenders are safer if they are living alone or with their families instead of in an approved group shelter program. Urge your members of Congress and the state legislature to create such programs.

Tell your state legislators that you also want them to make it possible for convicted offenders to get post-parole counseling from mental health agencies or maintenance groups.

10 Additional Measures You Can Take

To prevent child prostitution from reaching for your child, contact *Children of the Night* a private, non-profit, tax-exempt organization. For further information, go to their website at *http://childrenofthenight.org* Phone the organization at its national hotline: 1-800-551-1300. If you live outside the United States, phone the police and ask them who is doing the same kind of work there and help them.

While every incest case is different, there are certain characteristics many of them have in common: a dysfunctional marriage, a future offender who is sexually insecure, and a child who comes to be used as an emotional surrogate by one of the partners for the other. If you see such a marriage in your family, urge its members to immediately get professional counseling and restore it to health, or completely end it so the child doesn't become its next casualty.

If you want parents already trapped in incest to be able to get professional help, so the child can be saved from further harm as soon as possible, tell your legislators that you want the law changed so that no parent who comes to a professional treatment provider for help after the first time they lose control is given a prison sentence. The offending parent should be moved out of the home and placed on probation with regular exams by a lie detector and visits with their child only when a monitor is present.

If you ever have a child who has been sexually molested—or even threatened with being sexually molested—use any of the national referral organizations for abused children listed under the Readers' Resources section in the back of this book and take the child to a treatment provider so that your child isn't a further target.

Listen to several commentators to get the news about child molester matters, not just one, and see what your newspaper has to say about it, too. Call up some of its reporters if you have any additional questions about any story they write.

Contact the National Center for Missing and Exploited Children (http://www.missingkids.com/ and get on their mailing list.

Contact the League of Women Voters and ask to be placed on their mailing list so you can get their ideas for better laws.

Call your newspaper and ask what is being done in your state to give convicted sex offenders treatment before they come back to the community.

If you know anyone sent to prison as a sex offender, tell them to to accept responsibility for being there when they see their first counselor so they can get all the help they will need.

Ask your congregation to contact the police, state parole agency and county probation department to reach out to registered sex offenders in your community to see how they are doing and to encourage them to stay in recovery.

If you have any additional ideas that you would like to offer for the next edition's list, please send them to: jgoldenflame@sbcglobal.net or by surface mail to:

Jake Goldenflame
Post Office Box 424250
San Francisco, CA 94142

Full credit will be given to you in print for any that are used unless you ask to remain anonymous upon sending them.

About The Author

Just before the new century began, the United States passed *Megan's Law*, requiring the registration of every convicted sex offender in the country and dissemination of their identity to the public. **Jake Goldenflame** was the first to openly champion it as one who fell under it. (See: "Advice from a registered sex offender," *San Francisco Examiner,* August 18,1997.)

That caught the eye of California's attorney general and, shortly thereafter, Jake began giving interviews to the media in conjunction with his state justice department's public information efforts. When Megan's Law later came before the United States Supreme Court for review, his story began to unfold nationally as *USA Today* wrote up his life, *People* magazine did a photo article on him and he became a featured guest on *The Oprah Winfrey Show,* which described his work in helping former victims to heal while encouraging sex offenders to accept this new law.

E-mail and letters began to pour into him from all over the world, asking questions that only a person like him could answer: *Why was I abused? How can I heal? How can I stop offending?* And, most importantly of all, *How can I protect my child?*

OVERCOMING SEXUAL TERRORISM is his answer, drawn from his own experiences, the sex offenders he has met in prison, therapists and members of law enforcement and community corrections. It answers every parent's worst nightmare by giving them steps they can take in their own home to make their neighborhood into a sheltering fortress that will protect its children.

Megan's Law soon began to evolve. Within three years of its passage, the version in Jake's state was amended over 200 ways, causing it to become so complex that a layman's version was needed. For this reason, in 2000, with the guidance of his state bar association, Jake published the first web site designed for those who fell under that law, writing openly as one of them. (www.calsexoffenders.net) He not only explained the law in the average person's terms, but included a list of recovery resources, available world-wide, that anyone could use who is struggling against sexual compulsions. Several years afterwards, aided by a public defender's office, he added a crisis counseling page for any sex offender who has become a fugitive, with instructions on how to safely surrender to law enforcement.

In 1998, Jake took the same first vows given to every Buddhist monk (*jukai*), plus a special one: to devote his life to helping all those injured by sexual abuse. Immediately afterwards, he began a prison outreach project, encouraging incarcerated sex offenders to start working on their recovery before they return to the community. The year after that he conducted dialogue groups, as an admitted former sexual abuser, with former victims of sexual abuse at the International Forgiveness Conference held at the Findhorn Foundation, in the United Kingdom.

He subsequently participated in the Victim Offender Mediation Training Conference co-sponsored by the Texas Department of Criminal Justice and became a member of the Victim Offender Mediation Association, a restorative justice organization whose membership ranks include prosecutors, public defenders, corrections and law enforcement personnel, psychotherapists and counselors.

In 2002, Jake presented his website's "Ten Commandments for the Recovering Sex Offender" before the San Francisco Bay Area Treatment Network of the California Coalition on Sexual Offending and since then has been told of its use by sex offender therapists internationally.

In 2005, after being out of prison fifteen years, Jake returned to prison as a guest speaker, addressing 300 inmates at Dodge Correctional Facility, in Wisconsin. Two weeks later, he addressed the Chicago chapter of the Federal Bar Association.

Well over a half-century earlier, his life had begun in West Los Angeles, where he says that he was born and raised "with a bunch of movie studio brats." Almost all of his schoolmates had fathers who worked at the studios, in the sound department, special effects crews or as actors, directors or musical composers. He says that he even went steady briefly with a girl whose father won an Oscar. His last name is the English-language version of his family's original one, based upon their earlier occupation as goldsmiths.

He became a journalist in the U.S. Army, when he was trained to become a public information specialist. Several months later, he was the one who notified the press when remains of the Soviet Union's first space satellite, *Sputnik,* fell to earth near his army post in Alaska. "The story went global," he says. "I got phone calls from news organizations all over the world. That's when I knew that I'd always want to be part of the news business."

Upon returning from active duty, he began studying at the University of Southern California School of Journalism, later receiving his B.A. in Social Sciences and then an M.A. in American Studies. He was hired as a newspaper reporter on a community weekly, later moving on to becoming a member of the public relations staff at a national charity organization and then a vacation substitute at a citywide newswire service.

To meet the rising costs of marriage and a family, he left print journalism for awhile. But in 1968 he began what became a ten-year stint as the West Coast contributing editor of a film magazine for entrants in the technical side of the motion picture industry. In 1970, he wrote a book on rising radical tensions in America, *Guerilla Warfare in the United States* (Los Angeles, 1970).

In 1980 he began the study of law at Southwestern University School of Law in Los Angeles and received his doctorate from People's College of Law in 1985.

He has since become a tireless champion of recovery for all sex offenders and all former victims of sexual abuse. He is regularly featured by the media and listed on leading search engines, with articles about him appearing in such print media as *USA Today, People* magazine and in stories by the Associated Press as well as newspapers across the country.

He has been a guest on *The Oprah Winfrey Show, The John Walsh Show, The TODAY Show, The Early Show, Good Morning America* and is a regular guest on programs of CNN, Fox News Channel, MSNBC, CNBC and Court TV, as well as on radio and television stations in Japan, Ireland and Canada plus radio stations here.

His books are carried by Amazon.com, Barnes and Noble.com as well as by other leading booksellers and foreign booksellers offering them to those who speak English as a second language, giving his work a global reach. In addition, they have now been accepted as appropriate reading material in over half-a-dozen prisons in the United States where they are being read by convicted sex offenders serving their sentences.

Jake holds a law degree, a master's degree in American Studies and took his bachelor's degree in sociology. He resides in San Francisco where he conducts a prison outreach project as a voluntary community service dedicated to helping incarcerated sex offenders begin their personal recovery before they come back to the community.

Seminars based upon this book are available and can be presented by Jake in your community or before your community organization. To request fees and terms, send an e-mail requesting Seminar Information to: goldenflame@sbcglobal.net or a letter addressed to:

Jake Goldenflame, J.D., M.A.
P.O. Box 424250
San Francisco, CA 94142-4250

Notes to Other Works Cited

Introduction to the Revised Edition

"Tough residency law spurs debate on sex offenders," *Los Angeles Times*, December 15, 2002

Lawrence A. Greenfeld, "Sex Offenses and Offenders: An Analysis of Data on Rape and Sexual Assault," U.S. Department of Justice, Office of Justice Programs, Bureau of Justice Statistics, February 1997, NCJ-163392, at: http://www.vaw.umn.edu/documents/sexoff/sexoff.html

Connecticut v. Doe,—U.S.—, 123 S.Ct. 1160, 155 L.Ed.2d 98 (2003)

"Meet the child molester next door," by Janet Kornblum, *USA TODAY* January 29, 2003, Life Section D p.1, col. 2

"Out of the Shadows," J.D. Heyman, Vickie Bane, *PEOPLE* 3/24/03, p. 121ff

Chapter 1 The Making of a Predator

Joseph D. McInerney, "GENES and BEHAVIOR, A complex relationship" in *Judicature*: Genes and Justice, the Growing Impact of the New Genetics on the Courts, November-December 1999 Vol 83(3) at www.ornl.gov/hgmis/publicat/judicature/article4.html

Chapter 2 Theology of Sexuality

Edith Hamilton, *Mythology.* (Boston, 1942)

Robert Louis Stevenson, *Dr. Jekyll and Mr. Hyde.* (New York, 1981)

Swami Prabhavananda and Christopher Isherwood, trs., *THE SONG OF GOD: BHAGAVAD-GITA* (New York, 1972)

Chapter 3 Victims and Consequences

"Adolescent Brain Development and Legal Culpability," Criminal Justice Section, American Bar Association, Winter 2003.

p. 118 in *The I Ching or BOOK OF CHANGES*. Richard Wilhelm, tr. Rendered into English by Cary F. Baynes. (Princeton, New Jersey, 1967)

Chapter 4 The Man with Nothing Left to Lose

G. Blanchard, "Aboriginal Canadian Innovations in the Treatment of Sexual Violence," *The Carnes Update*, Summer 1997, 4-6.

Rupert Ross, *Returning to the Teachings: Exploring Aboriginal Justice*. (New York, 1996.

The Story of Joseph: Genesis, Chapters 37-50.

Chapter 5 Evil or Ill?

Hanson, R.K., Gordon, A., Harris, A.J.R., Marques, J.K., Murphy, W., Quinsey, V.L., and Seto, M.C. (2002) First report of the Collaborative Outcome Data Project on the effectiveness of psychological treatment for sexual offenders. Sexual Abuse: A Journal of Research and Treatment, 14(2), 169-194

ALCOHOLICS ANONYMOUS, Third Edition. (New York, 1976)

J. K. Marques, C.L. Murrey and D.M. O'Connor, (1984). An innovative treatment program for sex offenders: Report to the Legislature. Sacramento: California Department of Mental Health.

Patrick J. Carnes, *Out of the Shadows: Understanding Sexual Addiction*, 2nd edition, (Center City, Minn., 1992)

Patrick J. Carnes, *HOPE AND RECOVERY A Twelve Step guide for healing from compulsive sexual behavior,* (Minnesota, 198)

Anna C. Salter, *PREDATORS Pedophiles, Rapists and Other Sex Offenders.*(New York, 2003) pp. 82-87.

Comet, J., de Leval, F. and Mormont, C. (1999) Summary: Comparative Study: specialized and structured treatment of sex offenders in Europe. CRASC, rue de Merode 199, 1060, Bruxelles, Belgium.

Freddy Gazan, The Taking Charge of Sex Offenders in Each of the 15 Countries of the European Union: Legal and Therapeutic Perspectives. A presentation given at the 17th Annual Research and Treatment Conference of the Association for the Treatment of Sexual Abusers (ATSA) held in Vancouver, British Columbia, Canada October 14-17, 1998. Abstracts of ATSA. The Battle Without Borders: Confronting Sexual Abuse in Today's World.

Worldwide ages of consent, www.avert.org/aofconsent.tm

Age of Consent, from Wikipedia, the free encyclopedia, http://en.wikipedia.org/wiki/Age_of_consent

Michel Foucault, *THE HISTORY OF SEXUALITY, VOLUME I An Introduction*. (New York, 1990)

McKune v. Lile, 153 L.Ed.II 47, 536 US—, 122 S.Ct.—(2002)

R. Karl Hanson, Ian Broom and Marylee Stephenson, "Evaluating Community Sex Offender Treatment Programs: A 12-Year Follow-Up of 724 Offenders," Canadian Journal of Behavioural Science, 2004, 36:2, 87-96.

Chapter 6 A God for Sex Offenders

The Holy Bible, King James Version, Thomas Nelson Publishers, 1990.

T'rumath Tzvi: The Pentateuch. ("Hirsch Chumash") R. Ephraim Oratz, ed. Gertrude Hirschler, tr. (Booklyn, N.Y., 1986)

Webster's New World Hebrew Dictionary. Hayim Baltsan, ed. (New Jersey, 1992)

Gershom Scholem, *Major Trends in Jewish Mysticism.* (New York, 1974)

Louis Ginzberg, *Legends of the Jews.* (Philadelphia, 1956)

Ephod, See: *Ex. 28:4-40, 35:27* and *39:2-30* as well as the entry *Ephod* in *The Oxford Companion to the Bible.* Metzger and Coogan, eds. (New York,

1993 (and *International Standard Bible Encyclopedia.* Bromiley, ed. (Michigan, 1982)

Brown, Driver and Briggs. *Hebrew-English Lexicon.* (Peabody, Mass.,1996)

The I Ching or BOOK OF CHANGES. Richard Wilhelm, tr. Rendered into English by Cary F. Baynes. (Princeton, New Jersey, 1967)

Aleksandr Solzhenitsyn, *The Gulag Archipelago 1918–1956 An Experiment in Literary Investigation I-II.* (New York,1973, 1974)

Elie Wiesel, *NIGHT.* (New York, 1960)

William Alexander, *Cool Water: Alcoholism, Mindfulness, and Ordinary Recovery,* Shambhala, (Boston & London, 1997)

John Bradshaw, *Bradshaw on: The Family* (Revised Edition). (Florida, 1996)

Pia Mellody, with A.W. Miller and J.K. Miller. *Facing Codependence.* (San Francisco, 1989)

Susan Forward, Ph.D., with Craig Buck, *TOXIC PARENTS Overcoming Their Hurtful Legacy and Reclaiming Your Life,* (New York, 1989)

Robert E. Freeman-Longo, "An Introduction to Relapse Prevention with Adolescent and Adult Sexual Abusers." A presentation given at the 1998 Research and Treatment Conference of the Association for the Treatment of Sexual Abusers and published in its *Abstracts* of that conference.

W.D. Pithers, and G.F. Cumming, "Relapse Prevention: A Method for Enhancing Behavioral Self-Management and External Supervision of the Sexual Aggressor," Chapter 20 in *The Sex Offender, Vol 1: Corrections, Treatment and Legal Practice.* Schwartz & Cellini, eds. New York: Civic Research Institute, 1995

Solicitor General Canada. *Triggers of Sexual Offense Recidivism,* Research Summary: Corrections Research and Development, Vol. 3 No. 4, July, 1998

Chapter 7 Dancing with a Higher Power

William L. Shirer, *THE RISE AND FALL OF THE THIRD REICH: A History of Nazi Germany.* (New York, 1960) Pp. 322-323.

Sophocles, "King Oedipus," in *THE THEBAN PLAYS*, E.F. Watling, tr. (New York, 1947)

Homer, *The Iliad,* Robert Fagles, tr. (New York, 1990)

Based on "Personal Astrological Horoscope," Trine, Inc.

Chapter 8 The Polite Interrogation

The Essential Rumi. Coleman Barks, tr. with John Moyne, A.J. Arberry and Reynold Nicholson. (San Francisco, 1995)

Chapter 9 Sex Offender in the Community

Kathy Evans, "The Crime Society Can't Forgive." *Sunday Age* (Australia) 29 August 1999

Kathleen Ingley, "Scholar Suggests City of Molesters." *The Arizona Republic* May 2, 1999

Anne Rice, *Interview with the Vampire: A Novel,* New York: 1976

Fred S. Berlin, "Issues in the Exploration of Biological Factors Contributing to the Etiology of the 'Sex offender,' plus Some Ethical Considerations," 528 Annals of the New York Academy of Sciences (1988) at 183-192

The Oprah Winfrey Show, February 25, 2003

W.L. Marshall, et.al, "Treatment Outcome with Sexual Offenders," *Clinical Psychology Review,* Vol. 11, pp. 465-485, 1991

Marques, et. al, "The Sex Offender Treatment and Evaluation Project, Fourth Report to the Legislature in Response to PC 1365," Division of State Hospitals, Department of Mental Health, October, 1991, p. 5

Sheila A. Campbell, Battling Sex Offenders: Is Megan's Law An Effective Means of Achieving Public Safety? Seton Hall Legislative Journal, Vol. 19, pp. 519-563, 1995

Tracy L. Silva, Dial '1-900-PERVERT' and Other Statutory Measures That Provide Public Notification of Sex Offenders. Southern Methodist University Law Review, Vol. 48, No. 4, May-Jun 1995, pp. 1961-1994

Dean E. Murphy, "Justice as a Morality Play That Ends with Shame." The New York Times on the Web for June 3, 2001.

Jake Goldenflame, "Advice from a Registered Sex Offender." *San Francisco Examiner*, August 18, 1997, A-15

Nathaniel Hawthorne, *"THE SCARLET LETTER,"* in FOUR CLASSIC AMERICAN NOVELS, (New York, 1969)

Child Protection (Offenders Registration) Act 2000-SECT 10, New South Wales Consolidated Acts, **http://www.austlii.edu.au/au/legis/nsw/consol_act/cpra2000403/**

Queensland (Australia) Criminal Law Amendment Act 1945

Office of the Queensland Parliamentary Counsel

Sex Offender Registry Act (British Columbia, Canada)

http://www.legis.gov.bc.ca/2001/3rd_read/gov11-3.htm

Bill 31 1999 "Christopher's Act" (Ontario Province, Canada)

Sex Offenders Act, 2001 (Ireland)

Reuters, "Korea Puts Sex Offenders Online," 6:16 a.m., Aug. 30, 2001 PDT

http://www.wired.com/news/print/0,1294,46437,00.html

Scottish Executive, The Sex Offenders Act 1997 Guidance for Agencies

Sex Offenders Act 1997 (for England, Wales, Northern Ireland and Scotland) HOC 39/1997

Home Office (U.K.), "New Clauses added to the Criminal Justice and Court Services Bill at Lords Committee" ('Sarah's Law'), a bulletin issued by Home Office (U.K.) 19 October 2000

Author's Web site for fellow offenders: www.calsexoffenders.net (See: Foreign Travel Advisory on Home Page)

Pamela Podger and Manny Fernandez, "Santa Rosa Sex Offender Found Dead: Suicide is suspected after Megan's law alert," in *San Francisco Chronicle*, July 7, 1998, www.sfgate.com

Kan Kikuchi, *Beyond the Pale of Vengeance*. Rev. Jisho Perry and Kimiko Vago, trs. (Mt Shasta, California: 1998).

Chapter 10 The Healing of America

Community-Based Sex Offender Program Evaluation Project Report to the Legislature (1999), St. Paul: Minnesota Department of Corrections.

Karl Hanson, "Brief Risk Scales for the Prediction of Sex Offender Recidivism" (Research Summary Vol 4 No 5, September, 1999, Solicitor General of Canada

U.S. Bureau of Justice Statistics, "Criminal Offenders Statistics" January 14, 2004

P. Smith, C. Goggin and P. Gendreau, The effects of prison sentences and intermediate sanctions on recidivism: General effects and individual differences. (User Report 2002-01). Ottawa: Solicitor General Canada

Testimony given on behalf of the California Coalition on Sexual Offending to the California State Assembly Public Safety Committee hearing on GPS devices held November 15, 2005 in Sacramento, California.

Jill S. Levenson and Leo P. Cotter, "The Impact of Sex Offender Residence Restrictions: 1,000 Feet From Danger or One Step From Absurd?" International Journal of Offender Therapy and Comparative Criminology, 49(2), 2005 168-178 DOI: 10.1177/A0306624X04271304

LEVEL THREE SEX OFFENDERS RESIDENTIAL PLACEMENT ISSUES, 2003 Report to the Legislature by the Minnesota Department of Corrections. (http://www.corr.state.mn.us/publications/publications.htm#so)

Amicus Curiae brief filed by the Association for the Treatment of Sexual Abusers (ATSA), *Doe v. Miller*, 405 F. 3d 200 (8th Cir. 2005)

Amicus Brief, Association for the Treatment of Sexual Abusers, *Connecticut v. Doe* No. 01-1231 in the Supreme Court of the United States (2003))

Anna C. Salter, *PREDATORS: Pedophiles, Rapists and Other Sex Offenders* (New York, 2003). P. 97.

Mike Carter, "Bellingham suspect could face the death penalty." Seattle Times, September 8, 2005

Maureen O'Hagan, "Mullen pleads not guilty to sex-offender slayings." Seattle Times September 17, 2005

Mark Foley and Orrin Hatch, "Making prey of the predators," The Washington Times, published June 24, 2005

House Resolution 3132: Purpose.

Daniel Macallair, "Prisons: Power nobody dares mess with," *The Sacramento Bee* February 29th Sunday edition, 2004.

Connecticut v. Doe, 538 U.S.1, 123 S.Ct. 1160, 155 L.Ed.2d 98 (2003)

Community Reintegration Project Circles of Support & Accountability, Revised edition. E. Heise, L.Home, H. Kirkegaard, H. Night, I.P. Derry and M. Yantzi, eds.Toronto: Mennonite Central Committee Ontario under contract with Correctional Services Canada, 2000.

Evan Heinse and Richard Ratzlaff, "'Circles of Support' for Sex Offenders Include Victims," The Crime Victims Report, July/August 1997 at mcccos@web.net

Candis McLean, "Next step—a national registry," Report Newsmagazine, June 3, 2002, Alberta, Canada.

W.L. Marshall, D.R. Laws and H.E. Barbaree, *Handbook of Sexual Assault: Issues, Theories and Treatment of the Offender,* (New York: 1990) p. 122

Randy Thornhill and Craig T. Palmer, *A NATURAL HISTORY OF RAPE: Biological Bases of Sexual Coercion,* (Cambridge: 2000, p. 77)

Reader's Resources

Books

Alexander, William, *Cool Water: Alcoholism, Mindfulness, and Ordinary Recovery*, Shambhala, (Boston & London 1997)

Baumeister, Roy F., EVIL: *Inside Human Violence and Cruelty*, W.E. Freeman and Company,(New York 1997, 1999)

Bradshaw, John, Homecoming: *Reclaiming and Championing Your Inner Child* (New York 1990)

Bradshaw, John, *BRADSHAW ON: THE FAMILY*, Health Communications Inc., 1996

CALIFORNIA's Megan's Law The First Year: Lifting the Shroud of Secrecy, California Department of Justice, May 1998.

Campbell, Joseph, *THE HERO WITH A THOUSAND FACES*, Third Princeton/Bollingen Paperback Printing, (Princeton, 1973)

Carnes, Patrick J., *OUT OF THE SHADOWS Understanding Sexual Addiction*, 2nd Edition, Hazelden Information and Educational Services, 1992

Carnes, Patrick J., *HOPE AND RECOVERY A Twelve Step guide for healing from compulsive sexual behavior*, Hazelden Information and Educational Services, 1987

Carnes, Patrick J., *HOPE AND RECOVERY The Workbook*, Hazelden Information and Educational Services, 1990

Forward, Susan, *TOXIC PARENTS: Overcoming Their Hurtful Legacy and Reclaiming Your Life*, (New York,1989) trade paperback January 2002

Foucault, Michel, *DISCIPLINE & PUNISH The Birth of the Prison*, Alan Sheridan tr., (New York 1995)

Hawthorne, Nathaniel, *THE SCARLET LETTER* in FOUR CLASSIC AMERICAN NOVELS, (New York 1969)

Homer, *THE ILIAD*, Robert Fagles, tr., (New York1990)

Kikuchi, Kan, *Beyond the Pale of Vengeance*, tr. Rev. Jisho Perry and Kimiko Vago, (Mt. Shasta, California, 1998)

Mellody, Pia, et. al., *FACING CODEPENDENCE Where It comes From, How It Sabotages Our Lives*, (San Francisco, 1989)

Mellody, Pia, et. al, *BREAKING FREE: A Recovery Workbook for FACING CODEPENDENCE*, (San Francisco, 1989)

Morrison, Toni, *The Bluest Eye*, (New York, 1994)

Prabhavananda, S. & Isherwood,C., trs., *The Song of God: Bhagavad Gita*, (New York, 1972)

Ross, Rupert, *RETURNING TO THE TEACHINGS Exploring Aboriginal Justice*, (Canada, 1996)

Salter, Anna C., *PREDATORS: Pedophiles, Rapists, and Other Sex Offenders*, (New York, 2003)

Solzhenitsyn, Aleksandr I., *THE GULAG ARCHIPELAGO 1918–1956 An Experiment in Literary Investigation I–II,* Thomas P. Whitney, tr., (New York 1973)

Sophocles, "King Oedipus," in *SOPHOCLES THE THEBAN PLAYS*, E.F. Watling, tr., (New York, 1947)

Stevenson, Robert Louis, *Dr. Jekyll and Mr. Hyde,* (New York, 1985)

Tannahill, Reay, *SEX IN HISTORY* (Rev. Ed. 1992) (Scarborough House, United States)

Thornhill, Randy and Palmer, Craig T., *A NATURAL HISTORY OF RAPE: Biological Bases of Sexual Coercion,* (Cambridge and London, 2000)

Elie Wiesel, *NIGHT.* (New York, 1960)

Wood, Gordon S., *THE CREATION OF THE AMERICAN REPUBLIC 1776-1787* (Chapel Hill: 1998)

Yantzi, Mark, *SEXUAL OFFENDING AND RESTORATION,* (Waterloo, Ontario, 1998)

Zukav, Gary, *The Seat of the Soul,* (New York, 1989)

Journals

PROFESSIONAL COUNSELOR: Serving the Addictions and Mental Health Fields
Health Communications Inc., 3201 Southwest 15th Street, Deerfield Beach, FL 33442-8190
Website: www.professionalcounselor.com
Subscriber Services: P.O. Box 420235, Palm Coast, FL 32142-0235
Tele. (800) 998-0793

SEXUAL ADDICTION & COMPULSIVITY: The Journal of Treatment and Prevention
(Adapted as The Journal of the National Council on Sexual Addiction and Compulsivity)
Patrick J. Carnes, Ph.D., Editor in Chief
Website: www.tandfdc.com/jnls/sac.htm#top
Subscription Services:
Taylor & Francis Order Dept.
47 Runway Road, Suite "G"
Levittown, PA 19057-4000
Tele. (800) 821-8312

Websites

AMERICAN FOUNDATION FOR ADDICTION RESEARCH
Links to Web Resources in the field of addictions.
Website: www.addiction/research.com/

"How Do I Know if I Am A Sex Addict?" an article by Robert Weiss, LCSW,CAS, Clinical Director, The Sexual Recovery Institute, Los Angeles, Orange County. Website:www.sexualrecovery.com

Sex Addiction Screening Test of 25 questions with self-scoring guide to determine whether there are issues of sexual addiction requiring exploration with a professional clinician; link to list of clinics, therapists, publishers and some 12 Step Groups. (Online resource of Patrick J. Carnes, Ph.D., editor of Sexual Addiction & Compulsivity)
Website: www.sexhelp.com

CALIFORNIA COALITION ON SEXUAL OFENDING
5361 N. Pershing Ave., Ste. H
Stockton, CA 95207

www.ccoso.org

Coalition members are representatives from law enforcement, criminal justice, mental health, probation, parole and community services dedicated to addressing the issues related to sexual offending. Regional chapters meet regularly to allow members to network and exchange approaches and discoveries that may aid in reducing recidivism among both youthful and adult perpetrators of sexual crimes.

CIRCLES OF SUPPORT AND ACCOUNTABILITY (Mennonite)
#6 Trinity Square, third floor
Toronto, Ontario M5G 1B1

Tele. 416 596 9341

A community reintegration project sponsored by the Mennonite Community to assist convicted sex offenders being released from prison with reintegrating themselves into society while remaining self-controlled. Presently operates primarily in Ontario province but willing to assist other communities elsewhere in creating similar projects they can operate themselves through their own faith-based organizations.

NATIONAL ASSOCIATION OF ATTORNEYS GENERAL
News, Issues, Research and list of all attorneys general in the states and territories of the United States. Drop-down menu takes readers to a page listing their state's attorney general along with that office's phone number, address and own website.
Website: www.naag.org/

PRISON FAMILIES ANONYMOUS

A support system for families who now have or ever had a loved one involved in the juvenile or criminal justice system. Support group meetings available.
For more information, write:
Prison Families Anonymous

45 Prairie Drive,
N. Babylon, NY 11703
or E-mail: allanpfa@optonline.net

AAOR Online Recovery Group
Online forum offering support for those dedicated to recovery from abusive behavior: sexual, physical or verbal. A site to discuss your experience, strength and hopes in a life of recovery. Victims, Social Workers, Offenders seeking recovery welcome. No abusive language tolerated. To join this closed group, go to:
http://health.groups.yahoo.com/group/AAOR/

SATA-SORT

Sex Abuse Treatment Alliance promotes education and political action through its program on behalf of everyone affected by sexual abuse. Publishes newsletter, SATA-SORT News, four times a year, with contributions from offenders in custody and others. Also website at: www.sata-sort.org For more information, write:

SATA-SORT News
P.O. Box 1191
Okemos, MI 48805-1191

UNICEF (The United Nations Children Fund)

UNICEF believes that the protection of children is crucial to their survival, health, and well-being. Everyday millions of children are exploited, abused, or are victims of violence. Bought and sold like commodities, children are forced to be soldiers, prostitutes, sweatshop workers, and servants. Abuse, exploitation and violence, occurring usually in private, are often elements in organized crime and corruption. Only time reveals the consequences: children uneducated, unhealthy and impoverished.

UNICEF believes that everyone has a responsibility to see that children are safe. We work with individuals, civic groups, governments and the private sector to help create protective environments for them. Healthy, nurturing surroundings allow children to resist abuse and avoid exploitation. Caring environments fortify children against harm in the same way that proper nutrition and good health care fortify them against disease.

For more information, contact: www.unicef.org

VICTIM OFFENDER MEDIATION ASSOCIATION (VOMA)
Claire Harris, Administrator
2233 University Ave W, Suite 300
St Paul MN 55114
Tele.(612) 874-0570
FAX 651-644-4227
E-mail: voma@voma.org
VOMA Web Site

Center for Restorative Justice & Peacemaking
University of Minnesota
School of Social Work
1404 Gortner Ave, 105 Peters Hall
St. Paul MN 55108-6160

Tele. (612) 624-4923
FAX (612) 625-8224
E-mail: rjp@tlcmail.che.umn.edu
Website

www.calsexoffenders.net
The recovering sex offender's website. An introduction to the sex offender registration law, guidance in how to earn one's way back as a registered sex offender, crisis counseling suggestions and list of recovery resources worldwide for those suffering from sexual compulsions. E-mail link to author.

Professional Referral Organizations

Association for the Treatment of Sexual Abusers (ATSA)
4900 SW Griffith Drive, Suite 274
Beaverton, Oregon 97005

Makes referrals to qualified psychotherapists, clinicians and other professionals among its members throughout the United States and abroad who adhere
to its ethical standards and provide recognized treatment to sex offenders.

Tele. (503) 643-1023
ATSA Website
E-mail: atsa@atsa.com

The Safer Society Foundation
P.O. Box 340
Brandon, Vt. 05733-0340
Tele. (802) 247-5141
Monday thru Fridays
9:00 A.M. to 5:00 P.M. E.T.
A nonprofit agency for the prevention and treatment of sexual abuse that
also offers referrals to therapists for those requesting the same.
Web Site

Stop It Now!
P.O. Box 495
Haydenville, MA 01039
Tele. (888) 773-8368
Web Site
runs a toll-free confidential helpline open five days a week, 9 to 5, offering
information and referrals to those requesting the same

Sexual Abuse Treatment Program (SATP) Canada
39 Stirling Ave., N.
Kitchener, ON N2H 3G4

Offender Program and Survivor Program. Educational Groups, Process Groups, Partners Program, Referrals, Speakers Bureau. Special program available for federally sentenced women helps with reintegrating them into their communities across Ontario.

Tele. (519) 744-6549
Fax (519) 744-2172
Email: cjiwr@cjiwr.com
WEBSITE: www.cjiwr.com

National Adolescent Perpetration Network
Kempe Children's Center
University of Colorado Health Sciences Center
1825 Marion
Denver, Colorado 80218

A cooperative network of professionals working with sexually abusive youth in the United States and abroad. Facilitates communication among those treating children and adolescents who are at risk of becoming chronic sex offenders. Provides information and referrals upon request.

Tele. (303) 864-5252
FAX (303) 864-5179
E-mail: ryan.gail@tchden.org
Web site: NAPN

Self-Recovery Organizations

At least eight organizations exist in the United States, some with branches abroad, that use an approach based upon the Twelve Step program of Alcoholics Anonymous to handle sexual addictions. Their members vary from those whose compulsions are no more than "social nuisances," such as exhibitionism, to others who are addicted to compulsive phone sex, extramarital relationships, promiscuous relationships in public places, and worse (although most members I met have never been convicted of a felony).

Using the language of alcoholism and drug addiction counseling, they vary among themselves as to what constitutes "sexual sobriety," or addictive-free behavior, ranging from 'no sex of any kind, other than with one's marital spouse' to 'avoiding whatever each person feels is addictive.' Open to men—and women—ready to stop engaging in compulsive self-destructive sexual behavior and (in the case of four of these organizations) to the spouses, relatives or friends of sex addicts—they offer self-help manuals and literature, regular meetings for group support, and one-on-one encouragement by more experienced members plus, in many instances, a local network of members who can be called upon for help whenever it's needed.

Sexaholics Anonymous
Post Office Box 111910
Nashville, TN 37222
Tele. (615) 331-6230
Email: saico@sa.org

Formed in 1976, Sexaholics Anonymous offers help to those who have lost control and are "addicted to lust." Holding the most demanding standard among these organizations, SA defines destructive sexual behavior as *any form of sex with one's self or with partners other than the spouse*, and for the unmarried, *any form of sex*.

They condemn *lust* even with a marital partner, in masturbation or in sex in dreams.

Their program begins by requiring an admission from the new participant of being a prisoner to "a power greater than ourselves," even though each individual is also urged to see their self as being that power's active agent. (From *Sexaholics Anonymous*, 1989)

Support is given through group meetings, one-to-one counseling by a more experienced sponsor-member selected by the new member, and literature containing lessons learned by others plus the Twelve Steps of Alcoholics Anonymous as applied to sexual compulsion.

Each member is urged to:
    make a totally-honest self-inventory;
    give up the right to live a self-damaging life;
    pray for help to God, as each person defines that word;
    make amends whenever possible to anyone harmed, and to
    forgive those who have harmed the member.

Sexaholics Anonymous is not affiliated with any religious denomination. In its 1989 book, *Member Stories*, accounts are furnished by twenty members—who had belonged for at least three years at the time of their writing—as to what living as a sex addict was like, what made them change and what it is like to be in recovery, ranging from a woman—whose addiction drove her into prostitution and "almost incest" before discovering Sexaholics Anonymous—to a closet homosexual, a child molester, an ex-priest and others.

In its 1982 pamphlet entitled *Sexaholics Anonymous*, the disconnection from the rest of life that a sex addict feels, the intrigue he or she courts for thrills, and the overwhelming shame that follows are accurately reported. A twenty question checklist is included along with a statement of known results possible for anyone who wants to change that kind of life.

With branches in the United States and abroad, literature and a newsletter, and a Corrections Committee that works with prisoners, Sexaholics Anonymous charges no dues or fees at any of its meetings and respects the confidentiality of those who attend.

S-Anon International Family Groups
Post Office Box 11242
Nashville, TN 37222-1242
Tele. (615) 833-3152
FAX (615) 331-6901

As an adjunct to Sexaholics Anonymous, SAnon International Family Groups provides support and Twelve Step training to families and friends of sexual addicts, maintaining that no one but the addict can control the addict's behavior and urging others not to unfairly blame themselves for what the addict does. The emphasis is on helping those who are close to the addict recover themselves. Literature, in either English or Spanish, is available at nominal prices. Branch locations available upon request.

Sex Addicts Anonymous
Post Office Box 70949
Houston, TX 77270
Tele. (713) 869-4902
Tele. (713) 869-4902
Email: info@saa-recovery.org
Formed in 1994, Sex Addicts Anonymous is a self-help organization open to men and women who share a desire to stop engaging in compulsive sexual behavior. They urge abstinence not from all sexual activity outside of marriage, like Sexaholics Anonymous, but only from the kinds that *each member individually finds compulsive and destructive for them*, a far more liberal standard.

No dues or fees. Helpful literature is available at nominal prices, including the pamphlet *Getting Started in Sex Addicts Anonymous*, which includes a twelve-question self-assessment and a list of tips on how to cope with situations where one doesn't want to act-out, ranging from indecent exposure to engaging in prostitution to engaging in child sexual abuse.

Now located in various communities in the United States and in Puerto Rico, the organization also claims branches in eleven countries including: Argentina, Australia, Canada, People's Republic of China (Hong Kong); United Kingdom; Finland, Germany, India, Mexico, Uruguay and Panama.

The organization also works with prisoners by sending them self-help literature that includes how any of them may start a group with the assistance of a prison sponsor.

Sex and Love Addicts Anonymous
Post Office Box 650010
West Newton, MA 02165-0010
Tele. (617) 332-1845
E-mail: SLAAfws@aol.com

Begun in Boston, in 1976, as The Augustine Fellowship—to avoid contro-
versy—Sex and Love Addicts Anonymous occupies the middle ground
between the standards of the other two major groups for compulsives by
defining sexual sobriety as not engaging in *any sexual activity except "that
which would be worked out in a committed, continuing relationship"*, and
where none exists, calling for a period of sexual abstinence. Hence, under
this organization's standards, one need not be lawfully married to their
partner in order to live a sexually sober life.

Addictive behavior includes any sexual activity *or emotional relationship*
that is out of control and threatens to destroy the rest of the person's life. It
is, therefore, both for those with problems with a sexual addiction or an
obsessive emotional attachment.

Recovering Couples Anonymous
Post Office Box 11872
St. Louis, Missouri 63105
Tele. (314) 397-0867, (314) 830-2600
FAX (314) 397-1319, (314) 830-2670
Website: http://www.recovering-couples.org

To rebuild the marital or partnership relationship damaged by sexual addiction, Recovering Couples Anonymous (RCA) was founded in the late 1980's
for couples seeking a sense of intimacy outside of addiction or co-addiction
to drinking, sexual compulsivity and/or co-dependency. Employing the
Twelve Step program, parenting contracts and "fighting" contracts for couples, they hold meetings in some eighty locations in approximately twenty-
five states; Canada, England, Sweden, Trinidad and Tobago. A checklist of

characteristics of functional and dysfunctional couples, a newsletter, literature and an audiotape price list, is available, plus location of the nearest
meeting. No dues or fees are charged to attend meetings.

Sexual Recovery Anonymous
Post Office Box 72044
4429 Kingway
Burnaby, B.C.,
VSH 4P9, Canada
Tele. (604) 290-93872

Post Office Box 73
New York, NY 10024
Tele (212) 340-4650
Website: www/ourworld.compuserve.com/homepages/sra

Another organization that offers assistance to couples *or* singles where
sobriety is defined as not engaging in any sexual activities outside of a
mutually committed relationship. SRA offers a twelve-step program based
on Alcoholics Anonymous at any of twenty four meetings weekly in the
states of New York, New Jersey and Connecticut.

COSA (Partners)
9337-B Katy Freeway
Suite 142
Houston, TX 77024
Tele. (612) 537-6904

Dedicated to helping partners of sexual addicts, Co-Sex Addicts (Co-SA)
also offers a twelve step program. For more information, contact them
through the phone number and address listed above.

Sexual Compulsives Anonymous
Post Office Box 1585
Old Chelsea Station

New York, NY 10011
Tele. (800) 977-HEAL
(212) 606-3778 (New York City & International)
Website: www.SCA-Recovery.Org

Active both in New York and San Francisco, SCA offers a twelve-step program for men and women who wish to overcome engaging in sexually
compulsive behavior by adopting a more responsible set of sexual bound-
aries.

Is participation in any group really necessary?

"No one who has turned his back on addiction has lasted long without
'community'…We are co-dependent…nothing can exist alone."

- William Alexander, *Cool Water: Alcoholism, Mindfulness, and
  Ordinary Recovery*, Shambhala Publications, 1997

United Nations Convention on the Rights of the Child

In 1989 The United Nations unanimously adopted The Convention on
the Rights of the Child. It went into force in 1990, seven months later,
after the twentieth State had ratified it. Since then it has been ratified by all
States with the exception of Somalia, which had no government at the
time, and the United States. It has four general principles:

- Children must not suffer discrimination regardless of their race,
  color, sex, language, religion, political or other opinion, national,
  ethnic or social origin, property, disability, birth or other status;
- Children have a right to survival and development in all aspects of
  their lives, including the physical, emotional, psycho-social, cogni-
  tive, social and cultural;
- The best interests of the child must be a primary consideration in all
  decisions or actions that affect the child or children as a group;

whether these decisions are made by governmental, administrative or judicial authorities, or by families themselves, and

■ Children must be allowed as active participants in all matters affecting their lives and be free to express their opinions, have their views heard and taken seriously.

As UNICEF points out, in many societies children are seen only as their parents' property, or as adults in the making or as not yet ready to contribute to society. This landmark treaty places the care and protection of every person under 18 years of age—every child—as a priority for everyone, especially for governments. The Convention has established new ethical principals and international norms of behavior towards children.

It is comprehensive, the only one to ensure children their civil, political, economic, social and cultural rights;

It is universal, applying to all children in all situations in virtually the entire community of nations.

It is unconditional, calling on even those governments with scarce resources to take action to protect children's rights, and

The Convention is holistic, asserting that all rights are essential, indivisible, interdependent and equal.

Under the Convention, every child has a right to live with his or her parents or maintain contact if separated from either one; cross national borders to be reunified with his or her parents, and be protected from abuse and neglect by parents or care givers.

Every child has the right to special protection in situations of exploitation such as child labor, drug abuse, sexual exploitation or sexual abuse, sale, trafficking and abduction.

Every child has the right to a name and nationality; protection from being deprived of his or her identity; freedom of expression; freedom of thought, conscience and religion; freedom of association and peaceful assembly; information from a diversity of sources; privacy; protection from torture or other cruel, inhuman or degrading treatment or punishment, and protection against unlawful arrest and unjustified deprivation of liberty.

Every child under the age of 18 years is protected from being punished by death or imprisonment for life without the possibility of release.

There are six Articles in particular which impact sexual offenders.

Under Article 34 of the Convention, States are to protect the child from all forms of sexual exploitation and sexual abuse, and particularly are required to take all national, bilateral and multilateral measures to prevent the inducement or coercion of a child to engage in any unlawful sexual activity; the exploitative use of children in prostitution or other unlawful sexual practices, and the exploitative use of children in pornographic performances and materials.

Under Article 19, States are required to protect the child from all forms of physical or mental violence, injury or abuse, including sexual abuse, while in the care of parents, legal guardians or any other person who has the care of the child.

Under Article 32, States shall protect the child from economic exploitation and from performing any work likely to be harmful to the child's mental, spiritual, moral or social development.

Under Article 35, States shall take all multilateral measures to prevent the abduction, sale or traffic in children for any purpose whatsoever.

Under Article 36, States shall protect the child from all other forms of exploitation prejudicial to any aspects of the child's welfare.

Under Article 39, States shall take all appropriate measures to promote psychological recovery and social reintegration of a child victim of any form of exploitation or abuse and do so in an environment fostering the health, self-respect and dignity of the child.

States having endorsed the Convention are accountable for ensuring that the human rights of children are realized, and their progress is monitored by the UN Committee on the Rights of the Child, an internationally elected body of ten independent experts with experience and expertise in children's rights. Countries must report to the Committee two years after ratifying the Convention and every five years thereafter.

Since the providing of therapeutic treatment to convicted sex offenders now has a demonstrable record of reducing further sexual exploitation of children, it may be appropriate for the implementing body of this Convention to encourage wider development and application of the same within more nations of the world.

UNICEF, The Convention on the Rights of the Child

INDEX

978-0-595-38355-9
0-595-38355-6

Printed in the United States
53228LVS00004B/381

9 780595 383559